THE HEART
KNOWS SOMETHING
DIFFERENT

SCOTT COUNTY HU...   ...VICES
Government C...
200 Fourth A...
Shakopee MN...

D1446167

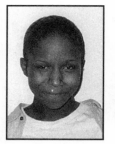

Jessica DeSince

Craig Jaffe

Shaniqua Sockwell

Angi Baptiste

THE HEART KNOWS

Anzula Richardson

Lenny Jones

Carlford Wadley

Wunika Hicks

Eliott Castro

Shameek Williamson

Lorraine Fonseca

Shawan Samuels

Clarissa Venable

Omar Sharif

Saretta Burkett

Kenyetta Ivy

Angela Rutman

Marcus Howell

Tieysha McVay

Paula Byrd

SOMETHING DIFFERENT

Teenage Voices from the Foster Care System

Tasheen Davis and Anasia

YOUTH COMMUNICATION
Edited by Al Desetta

Foreword by Jonathan Kozol

Mohamed Khan

PERSEA BOOKS   NEW YORK

In the following pieces, some names and/or identifying details have been changed: "Six Months on the Run from the BCW," "Sista on the Run (From the Past)," "Why Are You Doing This, Mr. Jones?" "My Group Home Scapegoat," "What They Say Behind Our Backs," "Kicked Out Because I Was Gay," "My Family Secret," "Therapy Changed My Life," and "I Won't Abuse My Kids."

All photographs of the authors are by Laura Dwight, except for the following: Jessica DeSince, Shawan Raheem Samuels, and Omar Sharif by Al Desetta; Craig Jaffe and Eliott Castro by Phil Kay; and Tasheen Davis with Anasia by Saretta Andrea Burkett. Used by permission.

Copyright © 1996 by Youth Communication ® / New York Center, Inc.

All rights reserved. No part of this publication may be reproduced or transmitted in any form or by any means, electronic or mechanical, including print, photocopy, recording, or any information storage and retrieval system, without prior written permission from the publisher.

For information, write to the publisher:

Persea Books, Inc.
171 Madison Avenue
New York, New York 10016

Library of Congress Cataloging-in-Publication Data

The heart knows something different : teenage voices from the foster care system : youth communication / edited by Al Desetta.
p. c.m.
Includes bibliographical references.
ISBN 0-89255-215-8 (hardcover : alk. paper). — ISBN 0-89255-218-2 (pbk. : alk. paper)
1. Foster children—United States—Case studies. 2. Teenagers—United States—Case studies. 3. Foster home care—United States—Case studies. 4. Group homes for teenagers—United States—Case studies. I. Desetta, Al.
HV881.H43 1996
362.7'33'0973—dc20

96-14
CIP

Designed by REM Studio, Inc.
Manufactured in the United States of America
First Edition

*This book is dedicated to the young people
who have risked sharing these stories
(including the many writers of* Foster Care Youth United
*who were not published here),
to their peers who are living in foster care,
and to the many caring adults who are working
to change the system, as well as the conditions
which make foster care necessary.*

KEITH HEFNER
Executive Director
Youth Communication

CONTENTS

FOREWORD *by Jonathan Kozol*   xi

INTRODUCTION   *xv*

I. FAMILY

QUESTIONS WITHOUT ANSWERS   3
Shaniqua Sockwell

SIX MONTHS ON THE RUN FROM THE BCW   9
Shawan Raheem Samuels

MY FOSTER MOTHER IS MY BEST FRIEND   25
Omar Sharif

I LOST MY BROTHER TO ADOPTION   30
Wunika Hicks

SHE'LL ALWAYS BE MY MOTHER   34
Wunika Hicks

MY CREW WAS MY FAMILY   39
Craig Jaffe

SHORT TAKES: REMEMBERING FAMILY   49

*Ishan Grant, Peggy Roedeshimer, Larita Bishop, Kareem Powell,
Laura White*

II. LIVING IN THE SYSTEM

MY DAY IN THE GROUP HOME   61
Carlford Wadley

FINDING A FATHER IN THE SYSTEM   64
Clarissa Venable

SISTA ON THE RUN (FROM THE PAST)   68
Wunika Hicks

WHY I'M BETTER OFF IN FOSTER CARE   73
Angela Rutman

CAN THE COUNSELORS KEEP A SECRET?   76
Anonymous

MAKING A NEW FAMILY   78
Lorraine Fonseca

WHY ARE YOU DOING THIS, MR. JONES?   83
Anonymous

HOW I BECAME A STRONGER MOTHER   93
Anzula B. Richardson

PEER PRESSURE AND ME   97
Craig Jaffe

KICKED TO THE CURB AT TWENTY-ONE   100
Rick Bullard

MY GROUP HOME SCAPEGOAT   105
Angela Rutman

A THREE-POINT SHOOTER   107
Max Morán

SHORT TAKES: IF I RAN FOSTER CARE . . .   *110*

Anita Nieves, Anthony McMahon, Brooke Montgomery, Miranda Kent

III. WHO AM I?

HOW I LIVED A DOUBLE LIFE   *121*
Omar Sharif

WHY NO ONE KNOWS I'M A FOSTER CHILD   *125*
Shaniqua Sockwell

KEEPING IT ON THE DOWN LOW   *128*
Lenny Jones

WHAT THEY SAY BEHIND OUR BACKS   *131*
Lenny Jones

KICKED OUT BECAUSE I WAS GAY   *135*
Shameek Williamson

MY FRIEND MARISOL   *139*
Angi Baptiste

IS STEALING MY ADDICTION?   *143*
Anonymous

PHAT FLOWS, HONEYS, AND THE BOOMS   *147*
Shawan Raheem Samuels

I'M THE MOMMY NOW   *151*
Jessica DeSince

WHO'S THE REAL "PROBLEM CHILD"?   *155*
Marcus J. Howell

SHORT TAKES: WHO WILL I BECOME?   *157*

Max Morán, Anonymous, Dhanisha Jarecha, Zerlena Ronda

IV. LOOKING TO THE FUTURE

FROM FIGHTER TO FRIEND   *167*
Kenyetta Ivy

STAYING WITH THE HURT   171
Tasheen Davis

MY FAMILY SECRET   174
Tieysha McVay

THERAPY CHANGED MY LIFE   180
Lenny Jones

HOW I MADE PEACE WITH THE PAST   185
Paula Byrd

FACING THE PROBLEM   190
Eliott Castro

A LONER IN THE GROUP HOME   193
Mohamed Khan

I WON'T ABUSE MY KIDS   197
Saretta Andrea Burkett

WRITING TAUGHT ME ABOUT MYSELF   204
Omar Sharif

A VACATION FROM MR. HOPE   206
Wunika Hicks

MESSAGES FROM THE WRITERS   212
Craig Jaffe, Wunika Hicks, Lenny Jones, Tieysha McVay,
Carlford Wadley, Saretta Andrea Burkett

GLOSSARY OF SLANG   215
RESOURCES   218
SUBJECT GUIDE   220
ACKNOWLEDGMENTS   227
ABOUT YOUTH COMMUNICATION   230
ABOUT THE EDITOR   232

FOREWORD

F rom the opening pages of this stirring book, readers will feel the shock of recognition that accompanies the first discovery of literary brilliance coming from a social context in which most of us, indoctrinated by the bias of presupposition, would not ordinarily expect to find it. They will also quickly understand that this is not another of those earnestly repetitive collections of "sad stories" by a group of "victimized" young men and women who are frequently presented to us by the press as "typical examples" of a certain category of low-income youth. Much to the reverse, these are the works of stubbornly unique, diversely talented young writers who share only the one common bond of living in foster care and having been encouraged by a group of rigorous editors—many their own peers—to share with us the mix of pain and fear, and sometimes hope, and sometimes even happiness, that their experience involves.

Among the more than three dozen authors represented here, several will inevitably stand out by force of sheer precocity. The powerful narratives of life on the run and in the streets, by Shawan Raheem Samuels and Craig Jaffe, are riveting and richly textured stories of the search for physical and spiritual salvation in the face of urban desolation. The four related pieces written by Wunika Hicks—a sixteen-year-old high school student when she did this writing, now a college student in upstate New York—and the opening story by

Shaniqua Sockwell demonstrate not only literary artistry but also introspective courage.

Readers, I think, will also be profoundly moved by Laura White's brief, haunting recollection of her search for her father, Tasheen Davis's confessional account of her dangerous behavior as a frightened teenage mother, and Max Morán's remarkable description of his solitary meditations during a subway ride to Coney Island. But to emphasize the contributions of these gifted individuals runs the risk of seeming to diminish many others in which longing, terror, honesty, and eloquence combine to seize the reader's heart and mind.

There is a magnificent variety of style here. Some of the authors speak in what newspapers call "street dialect," the best example being Mr. Samuels's powerful work, in which the vernacular is handled with a discipline and calculation that deliberately lead us into what, for many readers, is an unfamiliar verbal universe. "Digits," we discover in his writing, are phone numbers. "Peeps" are friends. "Flip a script" means start a fight. "Boogie Down" turns out to be a coded reference to the Bronx. "Steel" means guns. "Munk" means rob. A "crib" is an apartment. "Dead presidents," quite logically, are dollars. A glossary, provided in the final pages of the book, constitutes a kind of passkey to this lexicon for those who find it baffling, although I think most readers will discover that the text itself reveals its meanings in due time, as is the case with almost all good writing.

Other contributors write in conventional English, often highly polished and proficient in its phrasings and grammatical constructions, while many navigate adeptly between standard English and the vernacular, moving from one style to another as if choosing at one moment to accept the uninformed outsider, then stepping back again into the more hermetic mode that makes us struggle just a bit to penetrate the prose.

What do we learn about the current state of foster care from these young men and women? The most important revelation, at least for this reader, is that foster care is not the universally destructive institution frequently portrayed by journalists. Some of the foster parents that we meet are, undeniably, impersonal, incompetent, or inhumane. Others are generous and wise. The group homes in which certain of the older writers live, though sometimes grim, are frequently pervaded by a mood of camaraderie and loyalty and love almost as strong as in the most traditional of families.

Discontinuity, however, is a constant theme; and, as in a Dickens novel, virtually every period of happiness and safety seems to be the prelude to an episode of devastation and irrational decision-making by bureaucracy. While many of the social workers seem exemplary, there is an unmistakable impression here that, by and large, American society has written off the human value of the children and teenagers whom we meet. If there is one consistent message that emerges from these pages, it is a tacit recognition of the fearful equanimity with which a rich and clever nation can condemn a generation of young people to so many years of intermittent desperation for no cause beyond the sin of having been born to mothers who, too frequently, were once ill-treated children themselves.

The dominant theme throughout this book, however, is the power of transcendent moral courage in so many of these young survivors. The persistence of hope and the resilience of the heart, the longing to believe in human goodness even where it seems to be eclipsed by nearly universal scorn, is the ultimate redemptive meaning that pervades this work. The longing to affirm life in the midst of death, to choose love in the face of hate, has been described before by authors as diverse as Elie Wiesel, Viktor Frankl, Langston Hughes, and William Faulkner, and of course, in the words of Hebrew scripture and those of the Christian gospel. But there is a special miracle at stake when affirmation of this sort is voiced by those who are surrounded by the symbols of destruction as they speak.

Juan Bautista Castro, a poet living in New York's South Bronx, where many of the authors of this book were born, has described a child he had seen once in a film about the Holocaust: "We see her only for ten seconds, but we can't forget her. There is a light reflecting from her. It is like the illumination of the angels. She tells us, 'There is something in me you cannot destroy.' "

Readers, I think, will feel that they have seen that light again within the luminous testimonies of this book. "The heart knows something different," as the title tells us. What it knows cannot be summarized simplistically—because this book is not simplistic, nor is it didactic or dogmatic—but the knowledge gained by these young people has the healing qualities of gentleness and mercy and forgiveness. In any age, these virtues would be blessings. In the coldness of our present days, they have the quality of grace. For this, and for the other gifts these youthful authors bring us, I am personally grateful.

JONATHAN KOZOL

INTRODUCTION

I t was funny how we were in pain, but the world never stopped for us, it still moved on. I guess you could say it's just like the moon and the stars—you want them to shine forever, but then they disappear and you're left hoping for tomorrow."

With a direct and striking simplicity, eighteen-year-old Wunika Hicks describes the night she and her brother were taken away from their mother and placed into foster care. Although she could not know it at the time, that night was the beginning for Wunika of a ten-year journey through "the system," as foster care is universally known to hundreds of thousands of young people across the United States. As a young woman looking back on that bewildered eight-year-old child, Wunika touches on two of the central emotional themes that thirty-nine young writers explore in *The Heart Knows Something Different*—the pain of separation from family and the stubborn resiliency of hope for the future.

The teenaged writers in the following pages left their natural families because they were abused or neglected, or because poverty, death, illness, or other circumstances beyond their control prevented their families from properly caring for them. They write about losing loved ones but also about finding new families in foster care. They describe coming to terms with difficult childhoods and drawing strength from the past. After reading their stories we know how they feel about living in foster care, about preparing for life beyond it, and all the while, they give us insights into how the system might possibly be changed for the better.

Rarely have these experiences been told with such immediacy. Most books about foster care are either clinical accounts written by child welfare professionals, policy tracts by bureaucrats, or memoirs in which adult "survivors" look back from a great distance on their early years. *The Heart Knows Something Different,* in contrast, is a unique insider's record: it collects first-hand accounts by writers who are living in foster care right now and who are speaking directly to others their age in the same situation.

They were originally published for other teens in *Foster Care Youth United,* a bimonthly magazine founded in 1993 to give a voice to young people living in foster families, group homes, residential campuses, and other out-of-home facilities. The magazine's motto, selected by the teens, is On the Inside, Looking Out. These writers have broken through their isolation to speak to and for their peers. Through writing they have acknowledged and even shed their unease about being in foster care, and they now have a forum in which they can express complex feelings they've been holding inside for much of their young lives.

They reveal a world that remains largely shielded from public view for reasons that are both bureaucratic and deeply personal. That world needs to be seen by adults—biological parents, foster parents, childcare workers, foster care administrators, politicians, policy makers, and anyone who cares about our youth. Although rooted in the personal, these stories have a wider public accountability. The writers in this book are not venting or self-absorbed. They are trying to articulate and reflect on their experiences to reach their peers but also to speak the truth about foster care to adults. They remind us of our responsibilities to them, because after hearing their voices we cannot help but see them as individuals, lifted from the abstract statistics of "the system."

Since children without parents are a reflection of the vulnerability of families, foster care can be viewed as a barometer of our national well-being. The first orphan asylum in North America was founded in New Orleans in 1728. By the mid–1800s orphanages had spread across the United States, their growth fueled by the family dislocation caused by the Civil War and waves of immigration. In the early 1900s, more than 100,000 orphans and destitute children were living in some

1,100 institutions throughout the country, and between 1853 and 1929 orphan trains shipped many thousands of children from the East Coast to live with foster parents (and in some cases provide inexpensive farm labor) in the rural West. During the Depression, regimented institutions with hundreds of beds were the norm.

In the 1960s, a heroin epidemic flooded the system with children. More recently, the impact of crack cocaine and HIV and AIDS on families has pushed a new wave of children into foster care. (By the end of this decade, a projected 100,000 children will have lost their mothers to AIDS.)

In New York City alone, the foster care population almost tripled from 16,230 at the end of 1984 to 48,068 in 1993. The extreme stresses on the poorest and most threatened families are evident in the fact that nationwide nearly 460,000 children were living in foster care in 1995, up from 276,000 in 1985.

But while the statistics may fluctuate and the reasons for being in care vary, the experience of growing up without parents has remained constant throughout the years.

In New York City, the Child Welfare Administration or CWA (also known to many by its old name, the Bureau of Child Welfare or BCW) is the agency responsible for foster care. The CWA in turn pays scores of private agencies to care for young people in group homes and foster homes. This arrangement between public and private agencies is similar across the United States. Ideally, foster care is supposed to provide a temporary stay in a "homelike" setting before the child is either returned to family or adopted by a new one, but for many youth this never happens. Instead, they spend years languishing in the system without the love, attention, and stability they need.

Foster care, then, is too often assigned (or expected to accomplish) an impossible task: replacing the biological family. For children in care, the system becomes the Parent, carrying all the burdens and ambivalence of that role. The system can largely meet the physical needs of the young people it serves, provide food on the table and a roof over their heads, but whether it can meet their emotional needs is a question that is asked in a multitude of ways in this book.

Through their distinct voices we come to know these young writers and grow close to them, to identify with their hopes and fears. For Miranda "Nikki" Kent, fifteen, who lives in foster care in Alabama, the most basic wish of foster care youth is to have "real parents to call their own" and homes "where they can love and be loved in return." She adds: "I'm only a kid, but maybe by the time I'm grown there will be a better way and other children won't have to go through what my brother, sister, and I have gone through. Maybe all children with parents who don't love them, or who can't care for them, will have the chance to live as part of a real family with all the love and security of knowing that they are loved."

To best follow this search for family and security, *The Heart Knows Something Different* is organized into four parts, "Family," "Living in the System," "Who Am I?" and "Looking to the Future," each exploring a core aspect of lives in foster care. The book follows the path that most of these young people take: they grow up in troubled homes; they leave their families to live in a new setting; they begin to deal with the identity of being a "foster child"; and out of the turmoil of these experiences, they begin to overcome adversity and build independence.

In "Questions Without Answers," the story that opens the "Family" section, Shaniqua Sockwell looks up at the apartment building where she lived as a young child and is overcome by painful memories. But those memories have another side: "They have taught me a lot about the person I want to someday become." Shaniqua describes her loss of faith in her parents, who were ravaged by drug addiction, but her ability to confront that past also reveals her strength in facing the future.

In the section's second piece, "Six Months on the Run from the BCW," Shawan Raheem Samuels gives us a dramatic narrative of his family's disintegration. He runs away from home to escape a social worker who wants to put him in the system, and he ends up committing crimes. It is easy to dismiss this as a story about a "bad boy" and his gun, but it is better read as a story about a child who has aged too quickly because he has no parental affection or guidance, who has nowhere to go and no one to trust. Shawan writes, "A man who hates his family is a man who hates himself." Fueling his intense anger is his sensitivity to that dilemma. And the chaos of the story he tells had become a way of life for him by the time he began writing about it. Shawan would complete entire drafts by hand at one sitting and then would disappear for weeks at a time, reappearing to pick up his narrative as if he'd been gone for only a day.

In "My Foster Mother Is My Best Friend," Omar Sharif is finally able to call his foster mother "Mom" and accept her love after many months of living with her, but he can't bring himself to be adopted by her and wonders if he's made the right decision. Craig Jaffe in "My Crew Was My Family" ends up living on the streets, but he establishes a closeness with his peers that he never had with his adoptive family.

It is also in this section that Wunika Hicks begins to explore her past in the first of four interrelated stories that raise elemental questions about family. She recalls her shock when her only sibling is separated from her in a sealed adoption ("I Lost My Brother to Adoption"): "Was this really going on? I suddenly felt so protective of David. I hadn't wanted the responsibility of being his mother, but now I didn't want anyone taking him away." She questions, with a child's self-doubt, whether the adoption is somehow her fault. Wunika's next story, "She'll Always Be My Mother," looks deeper into her past with an unsparing eye as she considers the person with whom she had the closest bond and who subjected her to the greatest abuse. The divided emotions of allegiance and alienation that resonate throughout her piece also resonate throughout the entire "Family" section.

In the book's second part, "Living in the System," the writers take us inside the foster care system and give us an intimate view of day-to-day life there. Most of these stories take place in group homes, small residences housing twelve to twenty young people, decentralized versions of the impersonal and overcrowded orphanages of the past.

Here we see young people coping with the challenge of starting over as they begin to regroup and forge new relationships in unfamiliar settings. "My Day in the Group Home" opens the section with dark comedy, as Carlford Wadley maneuvers through an institutional maze characterized by mediocre food, odd roommates, and a frenetic routine.

We also learn that foster care can be a literal lifesaver for those who have been removed from abusive homes and who now begin to heal and grow in safe environments. Clarissa Venable ("Finding a Father in the System") learns to trust a caring male staff member. Angela Rutman ("Why I'm Better Off in Foster Care") discovers the structure and discipline her family could not provide her. Lorraine Fonseca ("Making a New Family") describes how she creates a new family through the friendship of understanding peers.

A recurrent theme in this section is "the staff"—the workers who have daily contact with the group home residents and who enforce the rules, strive to provide structure and love, and become the object of all kinds of emotions. It is an unfortunate fact that some group home staff and foster parents abuse the power they wield, and a system that is supposed to protect ends up having the opposite effect. This is the subject of "Why Are You Doing This, Mr. Jones?" an account by a young woman of having been raped by her social worker. The writer spent an entire summer working on it. She sat on a couch in our lounge, bent over her notepad, writing furiously, then giving it up, walking away only to return, engaged in almost a physical fight with herself to get it down on paper. But when she finished she was "a stronger person . . . not alone," and the response from readers was enormous because the story touches on a prime concern: the ever-present power dynamic between surrogate parents and children in great need.

Other stories about coping and persevering round out the section. In "How I Became a Stronger Mother," Anzula Richardson gets much-needed support from other young mothers in her residence. In "Peer Pressure and Me," we pick up Craig Jaffe's story again, begun in the book's first part. He has now left the streets and is living in a group home, successfully casting off destructive behavior from his past. In "Kicked to the Curb at Twenty-One," Rick Bullard shows the wisdom of twenty-twenty hindsight as he analyzes how the system could have better prepared him to live on his own after foster care. Rick reminds us that not all struggles in foster care are emotional: young people in care need to be able to find and hold jobs, secure adequate housing, and further their educations. Taken together, the stories in "Living in the System" ask an essential question: absent the support of the biological family, how do kids get what they need in order to grow up?

"Who Am I?" the book's third part, follows with stories that reflect further on the struggle to develop a positive sense of self and define one's identity in relation to others. It begins with a series of pieces that discuss a main preoccupation of many youth in the system: the stigma and shame they feel about being in care, and their need to hide that fact for fear of being stereotyped or teased. One particular worry is telling a potential boyfriend or girlfriend that they're in the system. The sense that one is "different" or "strange" and unable to communicate this reality to outsiders permeates these stories.

In "How I Lived a Double Life," Omar Sharif remembers how he "pretended" to be a "normal" kid during the day in school, and then was free to be a "group home kid" at night. In "Kicked Out Because I Was Gay," Shameek Williamson describes how she is not only compelled to hide her foster care identity from friends but also cannot tell her foster mother or grandmother she's gay because she may be asked to leave and has no place left to go.

But realizing they are more similar to others than they might first imagine, the writers also begin to react against their fears and see their foster care experiences as a source of strength. Lenny Jones interviews his classmates at school without telling them he's in foster care ("What They Say Behind Our Backs"), to find out what stereotypes they have about him, and then counters their often insensitive assumptions with humorous asides to the reader. One boy tells Lenny, "I think I'd try to hide it because I'd feel embarrassed not having a parent." Lenny responds: "We have parents . . . It's just that they're temporarily out of order. And what's so spectacular about living with biological family, anyway?" When another boy says, "They're just regular kids," Lenny answers, "Amen."

Other issues of adolescent identity that are not unique to teenagers in foster care are raised in "Who Am I?": a girl tries to understand her compulsion to shoplift ("Is Stealing My Addiction?"); Shawan Raheem Samuels illustrates, with a brilliant juxtaposition of slang and traditional language, the gulf between middle-class social workers and kids from the projects ("Phat Flows, Honeys, and the Booms"); Jessica DeSince describes her valiant attempt to be a good mother before her own childhood is yet over ("I'm the Mommy Now"). And in the final story, "Who's the Real 'Problem Child'?" Marcus J. Howell returns to the theme of stigma by demolishing, with subtle power, the myth that the biological family is inherently good.

In the concluding section, "Looking to the Future," answers begin to emerge to familiar questions. How can a difficult past be overcome? Where does responsibility lie? How can one move forward? Is it possible to learn from the past? Refusing to see themselves as victims, the writers understand that no "system" alone will provide the answers. They have been helped by peer counseling, social workers, therapists, and staff, but now they reflect on individual responsibility and choices they need to make. Here we see the roots of change, in some cases tentative, in others firmly grounded.

Lenny Jones, in "Therapy Changed My Life," describes his recovery from sexual abuse. He originally drafted this story in the third person but eventually shifted into the first person as the writing progressed, an heroic admission. (Originally published anonymously in *Foster Care Youth United*, Lenny has taken the further step of claiming authorship of the story in this book.) Kenyetta Ivy, in "From Fighter to Friend," changes, with the aid of an attentive and affectionate peer, from a violent and destructive person into a model resident. In "How I Made Peace with the Past," Paula Byrd shows courage and wisdom in confronting her dying mother with her anger, expressing her true feelings for the first time, a difficult but necessary process before Paula can then begin to forgive her. And Tasheen Davis ("Staying with the Hurt") and Saretta Andrea Burkett ("I Won't Abuse *My* Kids") strive to break away from family legacies of child abuse by coming to terms with the abuser in themselves. If the past cannot be left behind, the stories in this section display visions of a more productive future to balance the adversity of the past.

Each of the book's first three parts ends with "Short Takes," a selection of pieces that were mailed into *Foster Care Youth United* by readers from around the country (the magazine has subscribers in forty-five states). These pieces echo the main themes of each section and show the universality of the foster care experience, whether it is lived in California, Oklahoma, Alabama, or New York. The book's fourth section is followed by "Messages from the Writers," where several of the authors have a last word about what they hope to accomplish with their stories and this book.

Included at the end of *The Heart Knows Something Different* is a Glossary of Slang to help the reader with forms of usage common among young people today, a Subject Guide that cross-indexes, by story, the major topics addressed, and a Resources list to assist you in finding out more about foster care.

The process that has produced this writing deserves some explanation. One of the goals of *Foster Care Youth United* is to teach writing in a rigorous way, yet within a meaningful context. Our students' real-life experiences are not buried in a teacher's desk or journal entries but are published for readers in a nationwide magazine. Achieving writing of that quality requires the discipline of revising and rewriting through many drafts. Students come to the magazine as volunteers or for school credit, and work on these drafts with an editor in the same way all writers do. They apply much skill and tenacity to putting a public face on their personal experiences.

Wunika Hicks, author of four pieces in this collection, had a burning desire to write her first story about her younger brother David, the only family she had left when they went into foster care together as small children, and from whom she had been separated for years by his adoption. "I Lost My Brother to Adoption" took several months to complete (as did many in this volume). Although it is not an overly long piece, the emotions and complications involved in its writing ran deep. Wunika's first draft acknowledged her sadness over the loss of her brother but ended in a phony way, as she played down her anger about the separation.

Through many drafts, she rewrote the story. It eventually acquired a beginning: how, as a young child, she had to stay home from school to care for David while their mother was gone for days at a time, and how she resented him for robbing her of her childhood. Then a middle took form: Wunika's anger over David's adoption, along with guilt that she had been a "bad" sister for feeling resentful toward him. And finally an end: continuing anger that the system could "allow" her to be separated from her brother, and the hope that she might one day see him again.

That first story accomplished many things for Wunika. She began to let out some of her anger and she began to trust others to the point of sharing more episodes of her life with readers in her next stories. Each of these examined her past from a new perspective and with increasing narrative sophistication, as the disunity of that past began to take on a coherent shape. There were many times she wanted to give up or found it hard to go forward, but she stuck with it and completed her task as a writer.

Perhaps there's a parallel between navigating the foster care journey and writing about it. Both challenge one's ability to continue on, to avoid the false turns and the blind thickets, to find an identity, to complete the story. The writers in these pages have made that journey, and their narratives have given it a form.

In a sense, it is a journey all of us must make. Despite the secrecy and stigma that often surround young people in foster care, despite the extremities of experience described in many of the following pages, the crucial challenges faced by these writers are reflected in our own personal histories, no matter what kind of home or family we come from. These stories resonate powerfully in us because we recognize in them aspects of ourselves, the part of us that is attempting to come to terms with our own versions of loss or disappointment, as well as independence from the past and responsibility toward others. Like Wunika Hicks, who in the book's final piece "takes a vacation" from unrealistic hopes for her family, exchanging hurtful illusions for a more healthy reality, we are all challenged, to one extent or another, to give up those illusions. Underneath our outward differences from these writers, the primal issues of separation from family, finding an identity, and coming to terms with adolescence and adulthood are recognizable to us and therefore very much our own. This is the essential truth that underlies every story in this book.

We hope these writers emerge not as "foster children" but as

rich and multifaceted individuals who, because of adult situations beyond their control, happen to be in foster care. We hope each story
sheds light on a world that has been hidden and stigmatized for too
long. We hope *The Heart Knows Something Different* challenges
stereotypes and questions assumptions and helps adults who work
with these young people to better meet their needs.

And we hope that this book has an impact on changing foster
care for the better. These young people are simply trying to grow up
and mature and move into adulthood. They are asking us to recognize that basic fact and to understand how difficult it is to undertake
alone. Perhaps their voices will help make the system more respon-
sive, but they also warn us that there are limits to what foster care can
accomplish. They tell us, although not always directly, that we must
try to keep families together, to do all we can to keep children from
living without parents. They are asking us to think hard about what
we mean when we talk about the "best interests" of the child, to understand the full dimensions and complexities of that term. These stories, so fiercely truthful, are a tribute to those who have struggled to
make sense of themselves in order to help others.

AL DESETTA

I
FAMILY

QUESTIONS

What you had is gone.
Is it time to move on?

The love you shared.
What more can you bear?

Years are flying by.
Are there reasons why?

A part of life has died.
Should you cry?

Memories torn apart.
Where should you start?

—Katrina Foster, 16

QUESTIONS
WITHOUT ANSWERS

Shaniqua Sockwell

W hen I visit my biological grandmother in the Bronx, I'll sometimes pass by the apartment building where I grew up. When I look up at it, memories flood through me and tears run down my face. The memories are painful, and yet they have taught me a lot about the person I want to someday become.

I lost faith in the one person a child should never lose faith in: my mother. When I look back on the years I lived with her, I can see why I lost that faith.

I came home from school one day and found my baby brother Lewis on the floor, his cries unanswered. I picked him up and walked through the apartment, but there was no one home. I couldn't believe that my mother had left him alone! He was only a baby!

I stood in the middle of the living room trying to think of what to do next. I did the only thing an eight-year-old kid could do: I changed him, fed him, and put him to sleep.

Next I called my grandmother's house and found out my other brother Leonard was there. Then I sat on the couch and waited for my mother to come home, so I could tell her off.

Four hours later, mother came through the door. Her hair was disheveled and she smelled of alcohol. She was smiling. She saw me glaring at her and had the nerve to say, "Hey, girl, how you feelin'? I had me a good day."

"Yeah, I bet you did."

"What the f-ck's your problem? You better go somewhere with that attitude or you gonna get your smart ass smacked."

I ignored her.

"Do you know that you left your son home alone? Do you know where your other son is? I'll tell you where they're at!" I yelled. "Leonard's at grandma's house, and Lewis is in his crib sleeping. And you didn't once ask about them! Don't you even care about us?"

I was crying now. I'm sensitive about many things, but it takes a lot to make me cry.

My mother just stared at me like I was stupid. I saw no reason to say anything else to her, so I grabbed my coat and said, "I'll be at grandma's house."

As I was walking out she shouted after me, "You get your ass in this house right now, you hear me? I'm the motha', you do what I say!"

I looked at her and said, "Then why don't you start acting like one?"

As I walked out, I heard a glass smash against the door behind me and I started to cry again.

Soon I began to feel that everything my mother was doing—the drugs, the liquor, the fact that she stayed out all night—was my fault. Because I felt guilty, I began to act as if I didn't exist. I became very quiet and sullen.

The only people I would talk with were my brothers and my father. Basically, the empty space my mother left in my life was where my father filled in. He was home most of the time when she wasn't.

My father and I were as close as two people could be. He was the one who was there when I said my first words (which were *Dada*). When he had some spare time, he'd take me and my brothers to the park and the zoo. When I needed someone to talk to, he was there.

We talked about almost anything. And when I needed books, he was always available. He was a librarian at one time, and I love to read. The first book he introduced me to was *Little Women*.

My father taught me to respect myself and others as long as they respected me back. He taught me to believe in myself and never belittle myself.

In a sense, my father was my best friend.

I stayed away from my mother as much as I could, which wasn't hard since she was barely around. So while she was taking drugs, I was taking care of my brothers. I might as well have been their mother, not her. My father helped, but I had most of the responsibility.

One day I went into the bedroom I shared with my brothers, looking for a towel. When I finally found one, imagine my surprise when about twenty crack vials, along with a pipe and needle, fell out.

I immediately took my brothers and myself out of the house and over to my grandmother's. I didn't want my brothers seeing that mess, and besides, my mother would kill me if she knew I had discovered her hiding place.

Little did I know the crack vials were my father's.

I don't really remember how I found out they were my father's, but when I did it was too late to do anything about them. For the very next day we were taken away from my family. BCW* had found out about the way my mother neglected us. I was placed in a foster home and my brothers were placed somewhere else in the system. I was only ten.

When I entered the foster home, I got more love and respect than I got from my real mother. My foster mother treated me like I was her own child.

But I still loved my real father and brothers very much and worried a lot about them. I didn't know where my brothers had been placed, and I hadn't heard from my father or mother. I missed my father, but my mother was a different story. I didn't think too much about her while I was in foster care.

As I lived in foster care, I began to realize things I hadn't thought about when I lived with my real parents. I remembered that my mother had once tried to stab my father because he refused to let her go outside and buy a beer. Whenever she was drunk, she would take out her anger on us. It got to the point that my father stayed out of her way completely (except when it came to us) and I would pray for her every night.

It may seem strange, but until the crack vials fell out of that towel, I never had any suspicions that my father was on drugs. I guess this was because he didn't appear high or do anything strange—unless you count the number of times he was out of the house. (Don't get me wrong—my father always had time for us, but sometimes he was a bit aggravated and needed to leave the house for a while.)

But I realized that when my father was high, he never took his anger out on me or my brothers. He either stayed out of our way or out

*Bureau of Child Welfare, renamed Child Welfare Administration, and, most recently, Administration for Children's Services.

of the house. Although he used drugs, he was still a parent to us, unlike my mother. He once told me, "I'd rather die than hurt you kids."

Maybe that's why I didn't suspect anything—I never had any doubts that my father loved us. He may have used drugs, but he showed us he loved us all the time.

While I was in foster care, I never lost hope in my father. I respected him and believed his willpower was stronger than any drug. But after a while, I found out that he had been hospitalized. My grandparents didn't think that I should know about it at such a "tender young age," but eventually they told me.

Six months after he was hospitalized, I saw him alive for the last time. I didn't know it would be the last time. He had changed so dramatically that I was near tears. He was in a wheelchair and his proud African features had been replaced by scars and blotches. His kinky hair, that we all had inherited, was now replaced by smooth, manageable hair.

He could barely walk, and when I saw this, I excused myself and went into the bathroom and cried.

How could this have happened? I wondered. I despised myself for not being there for him when he needed me. I felt that it was my fault that this was happening and I didn't even know what illness he had. I was too afraid to ask.

When I turned eleven, the biggest shock of all hit me. It was a Thursday morning and I woke up feeling refreshed and in a good mood. I went into my foster parents' room to greet them, but they looked sad and remorseful.

"What's wrong?" I asked.

"Shaniqua, sit down," my foster mother said.

So I sat.

"Shaniqua, your grandmother just called and told us that your father died from AIDS."

My mouth went dry and slack, my hands felt like wax, and my whole body was shaking. I was trembling like a leaf. I couldn't even talk.

All I could say was "Oh" and walk out of the room. All I could think about was that I would never see him again.

The day of the funeral was dark and raining. Everyone who was close to the family was there. Even my mother showed up. When I saw her, I wanted to lash out at her: "You have some nerve being here, you even tried to stab him once! You don't deserve to be here, get out!" But I remained silent.

When I finally did start to cry, I couldn't stop. My brothers were there too and they asked me, "Nika, why you cryin'?" But I couldn't answer them. All I could do was hold them close and tight and bawl my eyes out. They were so young they couldn't understand that their daddy was gone for good.

The thing I now wonder about most of all is, "Why did my father do drugs?" It didn't make any sense because I never suspected it. Maybe he did it because he was pressured into it. Maybe my mother stressed him out.

It makes me so angry! Here he was taking drugs, doing the same thing he had told me and my brothers not to do! I wish my father had practiced what he preached.

The hardest part of this whole ordeal is that I will never be able to ask him why. If I had one wish, it would be to see my father again and just ask him that one question. I would ask my mother too, if she decides to come see me.

Losing my father hurts and still hurts, but I'm a stronger person now because of it. What I'm saying is that you never realize how much you love and care for someone until the person's gone. My advice to you is to not take your parents for granted, because they may be up and gone before you know it.

I want to become the type of person my mother couldn't or didn't become. I want to make something out of myself and help other people see that the dark side of things can also bring out the bright side as well.

It's been six years since my father's death and I'm coping with it and going on with my life. All of my brothers are in foster care and one is on the verge of being adopted.

I haven't seen my mother in six years. I think of her a lot every time my birthday and my brothers' birthdays go by. And even more at Christmas and Thanksgiving. I wonder where she is and what she's doing, if she ever thinks of us. Despite all she's done to us, I still love and miss her.

If I ever see her again, I will make sure to tell her, "Mom, I love you, but I've lost all my faith in you for reasons I can't even begin to explain."

My life seems to be going uphill instead of down, and I can look forward to my future as a woman and not as a little girl. But for now, all I have are memories and the words my father once said that I will never forget: "I'd rather die than hurt you kids."

❏

Shaniqua Sockwell was 16 when she wrote this account of her childhood. It evolved from separate stories about her mother and father over a period of several months. Born in the Bronx, Shaniqua entered foster care when she was ten years old. With three siblings adopted or in group homes, Shaniqua was inspired to write about her family after reading "I Lost My Brother to Adoption," an article by Wunika Hicks that is also included in this collection. Recently adopted by her foster family, Shaniqua plans to major in journalism in college.

SIX MONTHS ON THE RUN FROM THE BCW

Shawan Raheem Samuels

I t was a bright morning in the fall and all the young children and teens were leaving for school. I was supposed to be going myself, but I never went to school. My mother was trying to get me up in her usual way.

"N-gga, you better get your ass up. Do somethin', you stupid bastard."

I ignored her and continued sleeping. She was busy getting my younger brother and sister ready.

This was a daily routine for me. I would always act like I was gettin' up, but I would go back to sleep as soon as she left the house. Later that morning she returned home and scolded me some more. My mother always ruined my naps.

"Boy, I said get the hell up. You know your stepfather called those BCW people on me. They know you ain't going to school, and they told you a thousand times if you don't go they gonna put your ass in a group home."

"Yeah, yeah, yeah."

She stopped scolding me after a while, then left the house to go to an assembly at my sister's school. I dozed off into a deep sleep. Then I heard the doorbell ring.

"What the hell, is she gonna yell again? I'm getting the f-ck out of here."

I looked through the peephole to see who was at the door. I did it quietly so the person wouldn't know I was home.

Through the peephole I saw Ms. Johnson, that pesky BCW caseworker. She kept knocking as I tiptoed into the kitchen to get something to drink. She knocked for about fifteen minutes, then stopped. I dropped to the floor to look under the bottom of the door. Her feet were nowhere in sight. I cooked breakfast, then hit the sack. A half hour later a loud banging woke me up again.

"What the hell is going on!"

I walked out of my room to see if it was my mother. She wasn't home. It was someone ringing the doorbell and banging on the door, demanding to get in the house.

I crept toward the peephole and looked through. What do you know, it was that caseworker again. I crept away, closed the door to my room, turned the radio on, and went back to sleep. After a while I couldn't hear the knocking anymore.

I was awakened again, this time by someone calling my name outside my window. I recognized the voice. It was one of my peeps. I stuck my head out.

"Yo, what's up? What you want, man? I'm tired."

"Ayo, some honey was knockin' at your door with Five-O."

"What! What she look like?"

"You know what she look like, it was that lady who pops up at your house on the regulah."

As I suspected, it was my caseworker. She had finally come to get me with the cops.

I couldn't believe she had actually come to get me. I started to panic. I went in the living room and saw a note on the floor. It had been slipped under the door.

It said "Get in touch with me" with my name and my caseworker's signature on the bottom. I figured I better do the opposite and get out of touch. So I jumped in the shower, got dressed, and climbed out my back window.

I went to a friend's house to figure out what I was going to do. I knew it was time to leave the neighborhood and hide.

That was my plan. I figured I would be better off if I left home. I knew I wasn't going to school. I just didn't feel right attending school with no gear. My mother didn't have enough money to get me gear, only my brother and sister. She had stopped buying me things when I was thirteen. At that time I was fourteen.

Later that day I went back home. My mother was there, she had seen the note and read it. She said the neighbors had told her that cops and some lady were knocking at the door and I didn't let them in.

"You see, boy, I told you she wasn't playin'. You thought you was hot sh-t and now look what happens. That's what you get."

"Well, you know what, ma? She ain't gonna get me, 'cause I'm ghost."

"What, boy? Where you think you goin'?"

"I'm gone. I'm not going to no group home. She gonna have to catch me. She better have Five-O, 'cause it ain't gonna be no turnin'-myself-in sh-t. And if the cops catch me, I'm gonna fight them too."

"You need to calm your young stupid ass down before you wind up like your father, a jailbird for the rest of your life."

I ignored her and took the little bit of clothes I owned. I told her that I would check up on her and left. She continued to scold me as I walked out the door. I knew life would never be the same once we moved to the South Bronx, and boy, was I right.

My first night away was not so bad. I was chillin' with my friends around the way. I was lookin' everywhere, lookin' for cops. I was very nervous. I asked my Jamaican peep Bolo if I could stay over his house for the night. He knew the situation and said yes. He had his own apartment. I said one night would be enough, because when friends live together they sometimes become enemies.

Me and Bolo chilled and broke night. We stayed out drinkin' forties mixed with Guinness stout. Bolo was smoking blunts and offered me one. I had never even smoked a cigarette before.

Bolo worked construction and sold weed. I used to meet up with him at midnight when he got off the weed spot. Every night, I got the forties and the Guinness and we drank them together.

I started running out of money. I had just got a bonus check from a summer youth job for perfect attendance. The money wasn't much, so it was gone in no time. The forties were stressin' my pockets.

I was thinking, "Damn, I need money and fast." My man Bolo had funds, but I refused to take his money all the time. Once in a while I took the money, I ain't gonna front, but I needed my own.

Every day was an adventure with Bolo. He had me going all over, drunk and acting stupid. It was always me, Bolo, and my man Ant. We went to different parts of the South Bronx lookin' for girls. We were the hoodlum version of the Three Amigos.

There was always a girl for each one of us. Sex was no problem. I was always the shy one. Bolo and Ant were the loud rowdy ones.

We always carried condoms 'cause we never knew when we were going to have sex. Life was fun with these guys. The only thing wrong was that it was very hard to make money. There was only one thing to do. Ant's cousin was a drug dealer. His name was Cook. Cook was making mad cash. He drove a Pathfinder with Louis Vuitton leather interior. He hit Ant off with a fat rock. We broke the rock and started our own business. Cook cut us half of whatever we made.

I was making about $100 a night. It wasn't too busy around the block. It wasn't much but it was enough. I had dough but I didn't care too much about fashion, I had to eat and re-up. I also had to have money to drink mad forties through the night.

Me and Ant would stay out every night selling, then Bolo would get off work at the weed spot and meet up with us.

One night with Bolo stretched into a week. I had so much fun, it just didn't seem like a week.

When I went back to my house to wash my clothes, my mother scolded me.

"Boy, that lady from the BCW keeps coming here lookin' for you. That caseworker Ms. Johnson is a b-tch. She keep sayin' if I can't control you, she will."

"I control myself now."

"What you talkin' back for? I'll beat the sh-t out of you, smart ass. Who the hell you think you talkin' to? Where the hell you been? What the hell is wrong with you! Why don't you go to school?"

I walked out and went to the laundromat. I bought a forty. I ran into this girl Shantel. I had met her at a reggae dancehall called Dixie. Shantel was an older woman, she had her own apartment and a kid. She thought I was older than I was. She asked me why I didn't call her. She asked me where I had been. I told her I had a fight with my moms and got kicked out.

I told her I had just come from Bolo's house, that he had let me stay for a week. I knew she liked me, so I told her I needed a new place to stay for a couple of days.

She said come see her some night so we could talk about the situation. Of course I said all right.

Now I had to make some money. I couldn't go to Shantel's place with empty pockets. I went back to my house to put my clothes away and pick out an outfit for the next day.

My mother told me Ms. Johnson had just left. I got scared and grabbed my clothes and toothbrush and ran out the door. My mother yelled out after me, "You better get your ass home by midnight!"

During school hours I was making money. That's all me and Ant was doing every day. As I roamed around I started to hate my mother. She always yelled at me and never gave me a dime.

She was going to other family members, telling them what I was doing. Every time I ran into them, they scolded me. The only person I cared for in my family was my grandfather. When I went to visit him he gave me carfare, money, and always cooked a nice meal.

Well, me and Ant were out makin' dough. We were the only ones on the corner. I had to make enough dough to get me some forties and mad food from White Castle to bring to Shantel's crib.

Me, Ant, and Bolo went to Dixie every weekend. I'd get there about midnight 'cause I had to make dough for drinks. I was thinking, "Damn, I haven't slept in my bed for weeks." I was becoming used to it.

I was having so much fun. I felt free and no one could order me around. I followed my own rules. I did what I wanted to do.

We always broke night when we went to the Dixie. We wouldn't get back home until 9:00 in the morning.

As I walked into the club one night, I saw Shantel. She was like, "What's up, what you doing here?" She said I was gonna dis her by not coming to her house that night.

I said nah, I was going to come, but after I got out of the club it would probably be too late. She said that's okay, we could go to her house after the club closed. I smiled and so did she. She started whining on me. All I was thinking about was getting her in that house.

It was morning by the time the club closed. I went to Shantel's house. We were in the crib all day doing certain things. When I woke up it was evening. I got in the shower and got dressed. She said I was welcome to come back anytime.

For some reason I wasn't attracted to her. She was attracted to me, but I only liked her for her experience in bed and her apartment. I couldn't get serious. I tried to, but I was lying to her and myself. I never liked to use a girl, so I faked what I was feeling.

I had other girls on the low. Most of them were older than me. A couple of them lived alone. Most of them lived with their aunts or grandmothers. I was allowed to stay at their houses overnight. It seems that when you live in the South Bronx, kids are allowed to do what they want.

I was bouncing from house to house for weeks on end. I stayed at my apartment, Bolo's apartment, or different girls' apartments. My caseworker, Ms. Johnson, could never catch up with me, and she was very angry.

I made the best of the freedom I had. I made sure I never got caught when I was makin' mine. There was a little problem me and Ant encountered. More people were trying to compete. When we started making money, a lot of newcomers came to sell.

Of course we knew who they were, but they had never sold around our spot before. They were jealous because we were making more money. We had the good quality and the good quantity.

People tried to rob me a couple of times. For some reason I always got away. When Ant was around no one tried to rob me. Then one day Ant said, "You can't be running all the time. You gonna get caught one day. They always be strapped, but they don't shoot. But what if they bus' a cap?"

Ant said he was tired of these jealous n-ggas out there, and I agreed with him. I asked him what he wanted to do. He said he was going to get a gun from his cousin Cook, but we had to pay for it. I said whatever you want to get, we can get it. So we copped a .357 Magnum for $300. We chipped in and paid for the joint.

When we got the gun we felt invincible. I carried the gun and was just waiting for anybody to riff. When we had beef, we did what we had to do. Ant especially. He didn't care. If ya stepped to him, then you got what you deserved.

Once I got the gun I cared for no one but myself. I became ruthless. But for some reason I didn't get into beef. No one wanted to rob me anymore. I'm glad I had it like that, because I never would have fronted behind the trigger.

But I was depressed because I had no life. All I had was bullets, my gun, and crack to sell. I didn't care about jail or losing my life. I blamed all my problems on my mother. Any family member who scolded me, I hated. I would either curse them or ignore them. I was just another black sheep added to the family tree.

A woman always made me feel a whole lot better, but I never wanted to be romantic and settle down. I would always avoid falling in love. How can you fall in love without a heart? I was as heartless as the Tin Man in *The Wizard of Oz*.

A man who hates his family is a man who hates himself. I became close to an alcoholic. Every day, one forty after another. I wanted to keep myself alive, but I wasn't afraid to die. Since I had a lot of enemies, I was ready to die.

I felt like there was not a soul in the world who cared about me. I sometimes heard voices in my head telling me to watch my back. Voices that were giving me advice. I thought I was going crazy. I wanted to shoot someone so bad I began to shoot in the air and scare people.

I would kneel and pray from time to time. I would beg for forgiveness, because I was selling poison to my people, contributing to their genocide. I felt I was going to be punished for all the evil things I was doing.

I hated the drug dealing, the violence, the alcohol abuse, but I couldn't stop. Every day was unpredictable. I didn't know if I was going to go on living or get locked up. I woke up each morning happy that I was alive to see that day.

Sometimes I would visit my family, not sure if I would ever see them again. They asked me where I lived and what I was doing. They asked if I was attending school.

Of course I fibbed and said yes, not knowing they had already talked to my mother. They would always yell at me when I lied. My family didn't want to help, they only want to scold. So I took out my anger on people I didn't like.

When my family flipped on me, all I did was fill up with anger. Flashbacks of all the things that got me angry in the past and the present hit my brain at once. Memoirs of hate is what I call it.

Having a gun became an obsession. Me and Ant copped a 12-gauge shotgun and a .25 with a six-shot clip. Bolo left the weed spot and started selling crack again. We were all together now and we all had joints.

After three months on the run from the BCW, I started getting tired of hanging in Boogie Down. I was from the Boogie Down, but my heart was in Money Makin'. I told my boys that we should take some work down around my old neighborhood in Money Makin', where my aunt still lived, and make some money. My boys said let's go.

We went down to Money Makin' and brought some work with us. I saw all my old peeps from the neighborhood and all the gear they had. Manhattan brothers love to cop mad gear. I was upset with myself and ashamed, because I had nothing that looked new and dipped. Where the hell was mine? I would have rather had gear than money in my pocket.

At least I had my two peeps from the Bronx, Bolo and Ant. We all had steel. We chilled around the old neighborhood for a while. We wanted to see if there was money to make.

Just our luck, there were cops around. We got nervous. I threw up the peace sign to my peeps and we were out of there. I told my cousin that I'd be back soon.

As me and Bolo and Ant took that train ride back to the Bronx, I stayed silent. All I was thinking about was Manhattan. Bolo and Ant were snappin' on people on the train and talkin' to girls, trying to get the digits.

They kept asking me why I was so quiet all of sudden. I said I was tired and couldn't wait to get home. I didn't want to tell them I wanted to go back to Money Makin'. They would think I didn't want to hang with them anymore.

That wasn't true. It was just that I'm a Manhattan man and Manhattan is where I wanted to be. I never felt at home in the Bronx. We moved there when I was twelve.

We finally made it to the Bronx. As soon as I got to the block I grabbed a forty. A forty was my way of dealing with my problems.

About a month later I went back to Manhattan to visit my god-mother. She said she had heard things about me. I asked what she had heard and who told her. She heard I was doing bad and that's all I needed to know.

My godmother told me if I needed a place to stay I could stay with her. She said she would talk to her caseworker and try to be my foster parent. She had been a foster parent in the past, and was the foster parent of my godsister and brother. She was their biological grandmother, but their parents weren't fit to care for them.

That's just what I wanted to hear. I want to get away from the Bronx. I gradually moved into my godmother's house in Manhattan. My Bronx boys told me in a joking manner that I didn't love them no more. I laughed and was on my way.

My godmother explained that it was going to take some time for her to be my foster parent. She also told me I would have to go to school sooner or later. She said I could go whenever I felt I was ready.

Oh yeah, I took advantage of that. Sleeping every morning while my godbrother and godsister attended school. They had nice clothes and were doing good in school. I felt dumb because my god-sister, who was my age, knew a lot a more than I did. When I went to school we used to get the same grades, but now I knew nothing but crime.

Every afternoon I went to the school to pick up my godsister and hang out. I felt ashamed because all the girls I used to swing some-thing with were looking good and I looked like a low life. I was nothing but a troublemaker—the only thing I had going for me was my gun. People feared me, so they wouldn't insult me. I had a bad temper, so the insults never came my way.

My godmother didn't know about my gun because my godsister kept it in her room. For some reason, my godmother never searched her room.

Every day I had the same routine. Sleep in the morning, then go pick up my godsister. I had already been a month in Manhattan, four months on the run altogether, and I was doing nothing. I had nothing and I was nothing. I felt like I was surrounded by people who were doing something with their lives.

One weekend I was outside and I saw a crew of my peeps going to a ballpark near a local club. I ran to catch up with them. My godsister and brother were with them and I asked them where they were going. They said they were going to catch a munk.

"Who you going to munk?" I asked.

"The people going to the club."

"Oh yeah? Y'all be buggin'."

"Come on," they said, "let's go do it."

They would be catching leather jackets and shearlings. I needed a winter, too. So I ran upstairs and got my gun.

My boys had already started. They were smacking these guys up and taking their money and jackets at gunpoint. There were about twenty of us altogether. Everyone caught money. It was so easy.

Every weekend we caught something. We would start at midnight and rob until four A.M. The cops never showed up. We'd sneak it upstairs when my godmother was sleeping. Eventually I had three leather coats and a $250 watch.

My godsister always covered for me. She told my godmother that my grandfather bought the stuff for me. My godmother knew that my grandfather always bought me nice things in the past, so I got away with murder.

Now that I had money for my forties and a little gear, I was straight. The expensive coats made up for the little gear I had. Money was a sure thing once the weekend came.

We had guns and mad heads. People who were striving to have what you had. Even if you were a hood you got robbed, especially if you had something expensive. I didn't worry about those BCW workers because they didn't know where the hell I was. I stopped going to the Bronx and I told my mother nothing about where I was living.

I was very nervous because it was too easy to rob people. I

was always looking over my shoulder for cops or people coming to
retaliate.

My aunt lived right across the street from my godmother's
house. She found out where I was staying through the ghetto gossip,
the thing I hate the most. She came up to me in the street one day. She
said she wanted to speak to me about something important. I knew
my mother told her I was on the run from the BCW and that she didn't
know where I was.

That night I went to my aunt's house. Just as I suspected, she
knew what I was going through. She knew I wasn't attending school
and that I was staying with my godmother. She said she wanted me
to go back to the Bronx. I told her I was on the run, as if she didn't
already know. Then she said if I wasn't going back to my mother, I
should stay in her house.

"Hell, no, I don't want anything from my so-called family."

"What is wrong with you? Why are you doing this?"

"I'm for self now. I have no family. I hate all of you."

Then I stormed out. I felt no shame for what I said.

My aunt kept trying to get me to live with her. When she did,
I would say disrespectful and cruel things. So cruel that she would cry.

My aunt knew the family was breaking up. She didn't want it
to happen. So much had happened to my family over the years and
now it was all coming down on me. I guess she didn't want to see her
nephew end up in jail or a casket.

I had been away from home for five months now, five months on the
run from the BCW. The months had gone by fast because of all the
action and adventure I was involved in. All the forties I had been drinking made the days go by quickly, too.

My aunt felt that if I wasn't able to stay with my mother in the
Bronx, I should stay with her. I was living with my godmother in Manhattan, but my aunt wanted family with family, especially blood family. I turned down her offer again.

I was going through tough times and I was holding a lot of
harsh feelings inside. My family always scolded me when they felt I
was doing wrong. I was a rebellious teenager with an attitude. My
family scolded me 'til I couldn't take it anymore. Some of them would
scold me even though they were just as bad as I was. And so I hated
everyone in my family.

But my aunt was determined to get me to live with her. I knew
why she wanted me to live with her so badly. She didn't want to see

another family member die. My grandmother had recently passed away. Her death was hard on all of us, especially my mother. But my grandmother's loss didn't lessen my hate.

My aunt tried for weeks to get me to stay with her. I refused every time. But she knew her heartbreaking speeches were getting to me. She knew she could reach the soft side of my heart.

Eventually she reached that spot and I surrendered. I agreed to move in with her.

I told my godmother I was moving out and thanked her for letting me stay in her house. She wished me luck and I packed my last bag.

I stashed my gun in my aunt's house without her knowledge. If she knew I had a gun in her house, I would have been gone with the wind.

I hadn't used the gun for a month. I hadn't even brought it outside. My aunt had gotten me back in my right state of mind. I no longer wanted to be a criminal.

She was buying me clothes. She was making sure I had three decent meals a day. I had gear and I felt healthy. I didn't have the need to sell drugs because I felt good about myself, because I had at least a little of what I wanted in life. Back in the Bronx, I had nothing.

My aunt was also a little more strict than the rest of my family. She wanted me in the house at a certain time. My mother didn't really care. No, my mother cared, but I didn't really listen. She let me do what I wanted to do. My aunt knew that I didn't want to leave Manhattan and I knew she would send me back to the Bronx if I got out of hand.

She was also trying to become a foster parent to me. I felt everything was about to go right in my life.

I was planning on getting rid of the gun soon. I knew my BCW caseworker, Ms. Johnson, was still after me. I wasn't going to let Ms. Johnson know of my whereabouts until I was doing something with my life. I had no intention of being sent to a group home.

Before I moved out of my godmother's house and into my aunt's, I registered for school. One morning I had to bring some papers to the high school and I had to bring my gun with me, because my aunt's young son was home sick from school. I couldn't take a chance leaving the gun in the apartment, because he was always snooping around and getting into things. He was sure to find it and play with it.

I went to school, took care of my business, and left. I hung around outside 'til dismissal and waited for my friends to get out. When they met me on the corner, I told them the good news about me going back to school.

They were happy. They said now we would control the school. They knew I had the gun and the guts to use it.

I told them I was going to change, that the gun would have to go. I told them this would be my last week carrying it. I would be starting school in two weeks. I wanted to learn and be a good person. I wanted to make up for all my past misbehavior.

They looked at me like I was crazy. They knew I was not a punk and were sure I would get into dirt somehow. In other words, they felt that I was just talking about changing, and talk is cheap.

When my friends left, I went to the community center and played some basketball in the gym until these guys I knew came in. I had someone take my place in the game so I could talk to them. They were drug dealers and they wanted to buy my gun.

They asked me why I wanted to sell it. I told them I had been on the run from the BCW for almost six months and wanted to give up a life of crime.

They laughed. They said I would always be involved in crime because of my attitude. They said my attitude was the cause of my troubles. As long as I lived in the ghetto, they said, I would be involved in crime.

When they said that, it made me wonder if I ever was going to change.

The drug dealers figured I had shot someone and that was why I wanted to get rid of it. I told them it was clean and they finally said they would buy it later that night. Then they left.

I played ball until ten. Then I waited outside for the dealers to come back with the money. I stood in front of a building with one of my friends. I was so anxious to get rid of the gun that I wasn't as alert as I usually was. I was talking to my friend, who wasn't paying attention either.

Next thing you know, here come the Boys in Blue. They crept through the hood in cars and on foot. They caught me off guard and surrounded me.

The cops showed me my bag and asked if it was mine. Of course I said no. There were about seven of them surrounding me. One of the cops opened the bag and dumped all my belongings on the floor. Out fell the gun.

A cop came up behind me and hit me in the face with his radio.

"Ouch," I said. It really didn't hurt. It's like getting a beating from your mother—it doesn't hurt, but you cry to get her to stop.

The cop wanted to hit me again, but I was cooperating. They frisked my friend and let him go. They escorted me to a police car. They read me my rights. They asked me questions, but I had the right to remain silent so I did just that.

They took me to the precinct and put me in a holding cell. It was a small and very dirty cage in an office the cops used to finger-print other criminals. I was alone in the cell. There was no place to sit except the floor.

All the cops were looking at me as if I were some type of zoo animal. They asked me if I wanted to go home. I said "Hell, yeah," because I had never been to jail and I was scared sh-tless.

They said they would make a deal with me if I told them who sold me the gun. I never snitch, so I turned down the offer. One cop said all right, then it's off to Riker's for you. I said I can't be sent to Riker's, I'm only fourteen.

They couldn't believe I was fourteen because of my height and features. They wanted to send me to Riker's so bad. They kept trying to scare me. They told me not to drop the soap when I got there. They told me to be sure to tie my sneakers real tight.

They finally granted me my one phone call. I had to call my aunt because my mother had no phone. It was twelve midnight. I told my aunt what happened and asked her to get in touch with my mother.

The cops said I would be able to go home if someone came and picked me up before 4:00 A.M. I was happy because I thought my aunt would be able to take me out.

"No way," said one cop, "your mother or father has to pick you up. Your legal guardian has to come get you before four A.M. or you're going to Spofford, buddy."

Then I found out from the cops that my aunt had gotten in touch with my mother through a next-door neighbor. My mother told my aunt she was coming. I was happy because I just knew my mother was going to come and get me.

The police explained to me that I was going to have to be in court at 9:00 A.M. if I was released to my mother. I didn't care, so long as I was home.

I waited and waited. It was now 2:00 A.M. Two hours to go. I was scared. I didn't want to go to Spofford. The rumors and reports I was hearing scared me, especially since I was used to getting away with crime.

Before I got caught I thought I was so smart and sly. I thought I would never go to jail. Now I closed my eyes and wished that I was home.

I pictured my mother yelling at me in the morning: "Boy, get the hell up and go to school!" I pictured Bolo and me drinking forties. I pictured me at some woman's house for the night. I pictured my aunt taking me shopping for school clothes. I even imagined that I was in a foster home instead of jail.

But when I opened my eyes, I was still in the holding cell. For some reason I believed in wishes that night. In the real world there are no wishes. When you wish upon a star, you don't get very far.

Finally a cop let me call my mother's next-door neighbor. I apologized for calling so late. The neighbor was a nice woman and we always got along well when I stayed in the Bronx. I explained that my mother hadn't shown up yet and the neighbor went to get her. I knew once I talked to my mother, she would come and get me.

When my mother came to the phone, she sounded like she was still asleep. She asked me what happened and I explained the situation to her, being careful about how much I said. I knew the police were listening.

"Are you coming to get me?"

"It's two in the morning," my mother moaned. "I don't know."

"If you come and get me, they'll let me go home."

"Okay," she said, "I'll try to make it."

She sounded like she knew it was going to happen, as if she didn't care.

"Ma, be here before four o'clock or I'm going to Spofford."

"Okay," she said, "I'll see if my boyfriend will drive me down."

Then she hung up.

I just knew by the sound of her voice that she wasn't coming to get me. I knew I was headed for Spofford. Yet there was something in my heart encouraging me to believe in my mother. I knew she loved me, that we had a good mother-and-son relationship despite all the problems we had.

But the other part of my mind was telling me that she was not going to come because of all the things I said and did when I lived with her. I figured she hadn't forgiven me for running away from home and seldom visiting.

I didn't know what to think about my mother. I didn't know what to think at all, plain and simple.

I tried so hard to keep my mind off Spofford. It wasn't easy with all these cops trying to put fear into my heart. One cop kept telling me to keep my back to the wall in Spofford. Another told me to keep my eyes open all the time.

They were really getting to me even though I knew what they were doing. They kept asking me if my mother was going to show up. I said yes, of course, because I didn't want to leave any earlier than I had to. I kept thinking as I sat in the cage. Thinking of all the things I did in the past and got away with. Now this was the payback.

We waited and waited. It was now five minutes before 4:00. My aunt called the precinct again to see if my mom had showed up. She was upset to hear that she hadn't. The police even waited until 4:15.

Hate flowed through my mind because I knew my mother had gone back to sleep. She had enough time to get dressed, play a full court, and get down to the precinct. I couldn't believe my mother had left her first child in jail, just to catch a few more hours of sleep. She didn't give a damn about me.

Epilogue

I was taken to the Spofford Juvenile Detention Center in the Bronx and arraigned later that morning on the gun charge. At the arraignment, my lawyer said my family was waiting for me in the courtroom. I thought that meant my mother and sisters and brothers, but only my aunt was there. I was held in Spofford for a month.

Eventually I pleaded guilty to the gun charge and was sentenced to one year of probation. I was ordered to attend an alternative to detention program to get my grades up. Then I enrolled in a public high school.

I stayed in the Bronx for a few months but then moved back to Manhattan. I stayed out of mischief for a while, but not too long.

My Spofford visit made me more careful in the streets. I watched for cops carefully and tried to limit the crime I did, but through the years I have been arrested again.

I'm now nineteen. I still see Bolo and Ant once in a while. I keep in touch with my mother and all my family. I've never asked my mother why she didn't pick me up at the precinct that night.

❏

Shawan Raheem Samuels, 18 when he started this piece, grew up in the Chelsea projects in Manhattan and moved to the South Bronx as a young boy. With a mother addicted to drugs and a father incarcerated for long periods of time, Shawan was forced to deal with harsh realities of the streets. Since writing this story, he has been trying to earn his high school equivalency diploma.

MY FOSTER MOTHER IS MY BEST FRIEND

Omar Sharif

My foster mother, Ms. Bradley, taught me more than my own blood mother. Through her I learned how to cope with my emotions and how to deal with life. I think it was God's intention for me to live with her and have a learning experience that stays with me to this day.

I moved in with Ms. Bradley a couple of days before my thirteenth birthday. Previously, I had been living with my aunt and uncle in Queens, and before that I had spent three years in a group home.

My agency felt that my aunt and uncle couldn't provide me with a stable family situation and that it would be a good idea for me to live with a foster family. I wasn't too pleased about that because I wanted to stay with my aunt and uncle, but I didn't have any choice in the matter.

When I first moved in with Ms. Bradley I couldn't accept her as my foster mother. I didn't want to let another woman come into my life and pretend to be my mother. As far as I was concerned my aunt was my mother, because my real mother had abandoned me when I was two months old and I'd only seen her twice since I was born.

So I entered Ms. Bradley's house with a very low self-esteem. I was a lost person. I had been bounced around from my family to the system and back again many times. I couldn't admit my anger to anyone because I didn't think that anyone could understand. But Ms. Bradley understood.

There was another foster child living with us named Matthew. Every morning after Matthew and I got dressed and ate breakfast, Ms. Bradley made us stand in front of the mirror in our bedroom and say out loud that we loved ourselves. Then she made us give ourselves a pat on the back and hug ourselves.

Matthew thought Ms. Bradley was nuts. He had enough on his mind to be bothered with hugging himself and patting himself on the back. He used to get in trouble every morning because he would have a very nasty attitude about it, and Ms. Bradley would always make him do it over.

Me, I was good. I thought the whole thing was silly, but I couldn't see getting in trouble because I didn't hug myself.

It sounds funny, but each morning I went off to school in a good mood and came home in a good mood. After a couple of weeks I came to understand what Ms. Bradley was doing. She was teaching us how to love ourselves, how to build our self-confidence. I began to feel better about myself.

She helped improve our self-esteem in other ways. For example, whenever Matthew and I said, "I think I can" (which we used to say often), Ms. Bradley corrected us and made us say, "I *know* I can." She wanted us to have faith in ourselves. It feels better to "know" you can do something rather than "think" you can do something.

I felt loved by the way she hugged me and showed concern for my well-being. She took care of me as if I was her own. I didn't have the sense that I was taking up space in Ms. Bradley's house.

When I lived with my aunt and uncle I had every material thing, but I didn't have real love. My aunt and uncle couldn't relate to my pain because they didn't want to take the time to understand and help me. But Ms. Bradley's love was genuine.

Once I sensed she loved me, I began to trust her. I started to open up. I wasn't afraid of getting hurt by her because now I felt comfortable. As the first year went by, I slowly began to accept her.

We would have long conversations together every night. Ms. Bradley said, "You can come and talk to me about anything, anytime. You don't have to worry about holding back your feelings, because I can understand."

We didn't have to have a reason to talk. We'd talk like best friends talk. I told her everything about my life and she would tell me everything about hers. She tried to help me benefit from her experience.

We respected one another because we both had similar backgrounds when it came to our parents. She had a rough childhood, just like me. Her mother didn't want her, just like mine didn't want me.

The only difference was that Ms. Bradley hadn't been in foster care when she was a child. She lived with other family members. I guess that's one reason why she never pushed me into calling her "mom." She knew what it was like not to have your real mother. She said that whatever I decided to call her would be just fine.

Everything I was going through, Ms. Bradley had already gone through. She always seemed to know the reason why I did certain things.

If I acted out in school, she would say to me, "Omar, I know how you feel, I went through the same thing myself. I know where you're coming from. You're upset because you want to be with your parents. That's why you're acting out, because you have no one else to take it out on."

I would look at her and say to myself, *How does she know what I'm going through?* Then I'd go to my room and think about what she said. When I came back, I'd say to her, "You know, you're right."

I used to rebel against everyone who wanted to get close to me. I had been hurt by a lot of people, so I had made up my mind never to get hurt again. Ms. Bradley felt the same exact way when she was my age.

I lived with her for about eight months before I finally called her mom. The first time I called her that, the look on her face was like the moon shining. It wasn't all that hard calling her mom. When that happened, we both knew I had finally accepted her.

I lived with Ms. Bradley for three years. During those three years I became a happier person as my self-esteem grew. But when I was sixteen, the time came when I had to choose between going back home to my aunt and uncle or getting adopted by Ms. Bradley.

Ms. Bradley wasn't pressuring me to get adopted and she wasn't insisting that I go. If she adopted me, I would still have full contact and visitation with my aunt and uncle. The choice was mine to make.

I remember one thing Ms. Bradley told me before I made my decision. She said, "Omar, if you leave, I'm still gonna love you like my own, but you know that once you go, you can't come back."

It hurt inside to know that if I went home to my family and messed up, I couldn't have a second chance to come back to live with her.

I didn't understand why she said this, but through writing in my journal I answered my question. You can't come into someone's life, have a heavy impact on them, leave, and then come back whenever you decide. I thought what Ms. Bradley said was fair, because I wouldn't want anyone doing that to me.

I finally decided to go back home to my aunt and uncle, even though everyone was telling me it wouldn't work out. Although I loved Ms. Bradley, I was scared to get adopted. I always had my heart set on going back home to my aunt and uncle and this was my final chance to be with them. I wanted to give it a shot. I felt like I had to prove I could make it with my own family. Ms. Bradley was very understanding and respected my decision.

But I felt so empty as I was packing up my clothes, because she had helped me buy some of them.

After I left, I used to wonder, "Omar, did you make the right decision by deciding to go back home to your aunt and uncle?"

For a long time I couldn't answer that question, but now, looking back, I know I made a big mistake. When I got home to my aunt and uncle, I realized I had grown into a new person with Ms. Bradley. I had changed, but my aunt and uncle hadn't.

I needed a certain kind of love that my family couldn't give me. I couldn't go to my aunt and uncle with my problems. I couldn't be friends with them, like I could with Ms. Bradley. I wanted to go back to her, but I couldn't tell my family that.

I realized Ms. Bradley was the mother that I had always wanted, the family I never had. I wanted both Ms. Bradley and my family, but sometimes you can't have both things.

There was so much tension with my aunt and uncle that I got kicked out of their house a year after I returned. I ended up being bounced from group home to group home for a whole summer before I finally moved in with other relatives.

I don't blame anyone for what happened because it was my decision to go back home. I should have listened to what everyone was saying, but I was too blind to see what they were talking about.

Ms. Bradley is deceased today and it hurts to know that she is gone physically, that I can never see that smile and or hear that laugh again. I no longer have her to talk to when I need some advice or when I do something wrong.

She's not around to tell me the reasons why I behave the way I do, so I can learn how to change. I don't have her shoulder to cry on anymore, and I don't have my best friend.

But she is forever in my heart and soul and in every footstep I take. I feel that we are closer now than we ever were before. Maybe not physically, but spiritually. I can sometimes feel her guiding me through all the rough spots as I come upon them. She was and is a blessing to me.

Without her, I would still be just another lost kid in the system.

Love you, Mom.

Your son, Omar.

❑

Omar Sharif, 20, was born in Manhattan and, by his teenage years, had been back and forth between relatives, group homes, and foster homes numerous times. "Being away from home and from my family all those years," he writes, "made me a real strong person." A recent high school graduate, Omar studied to be a plumber, but is now planning to go back to college.

I LOST MY BROTHER
TO ADOPTION

Wunika Hicks

When I was just eight years old, I became a mother to my brother. I had to stay home all day to take care of David, who wasn't even a year old. My mother was never home. She'd be out trying to find a job, to make some money so we could have a decent meal. My father had passed away when I was two.

So I had to do everything my mother couldn't do—make David's bottles, change his Pampers (yuk!), wash him, and rock him to sleep. I'm surprised I didn't get left back because I hardly went to school. Do you know how it feels to look out the window in the morning and see other kids with their book bags while you're stuck in the house?

I really began to dislike David. I felt that if he had never been born I wouldn't have this responsibility. I felt it was his fault that I was restricted from doing the things that every young child wants to do.

So it was a relief in a way when my brother and I were placed in a foster home. I was turning nine years old and my brother was fifteen months. We were taken away because of my mother's neglect.

I didn't want to be separated from my mother. She tried so hard to keep us together. But on the other hand I was happy that I could go to school on a regular basis and play in the park with children my own age, since my foster parents would now take care of David.

Still, I hated being around my brother. I wanted him out of my sight. I treated David so badly. He wanted me to play with him or take him to the store because I had been more of a mother to him than our real mother. But although he wanted my attention I ignored him or pushed him away, because all I could see was the past, those endless days when I was stuck with him in the house.

When my foster mother saw the way I treated David, she would say to me, "One day you're going to wish you had a brother." But I didn't pay her any mind.

Eventually I moved into a new foster home. I was thirteen. I was hurt when I left my old foster family because I had been with them for almost five years, but the new home turned out to be much better. They treated me like their own. In the meantime, David stayed with our old foster family.

It wasn't long before my social worker told me my brother, now age six, would be moving into a new foster home, too. But there was a twist: the social worker said that my brother's new foster parents wanted to adopt him.

When she told me this, I stood up and just walked around the room. I was in complete shock. My body was numb and I began to cry. Was this really going on? I suddenly felt so protective of David. I hadn't wanted the responsibility of being his mother, but now I didn't want anyone taking him away.

I felt it was my fault that he was being adopted. I felt the past was coming back to haunt me. I wanted David now, but when I had him I rejected him. All I could hear was my old foster mother saying, *"One day you're going to wish you had a brother."*

I asked my social worker if I could still see David after he was adopted. She told me that his new parents would make that decision. She also told me that they wanted to change my brother's name—not only his last name, but his first name too.

"How can they do this?" I asked the social worker. "What gives them that right? I took care of him. I'm more of a mother to him than anyone could ever be. I know what he likes and dislikes. I'm his mother, I'm his sister, I'm everything to him! I'm all the family he has—me, not some strangers!"

The social worker just looked at me. She could see the pain I was going through, but all she could say was, "That's the law."

I asked my social worker to find out if they'd allow me to see David. She said a good time for a visit would be around the Christmas vacation, if the adoptive parents agreed. I was happy that I'd finally get to see him.

But before the visit could be arranged, my social worker transferred to a different department. Later I found out that the adoptive parents never even answered my request for visitation rights.

A few months later I got a new social worker, but she didn't care that I missed my brother. All she did was sit there and smoke. Pretty soon, she left too.

(I can't help but think that if I hadn't been running from social worker to social worker, I might have been able to see my brother by now. I've been in foster care for eight years and I think I've had six social workers, five law guardians, and counting.)

The third social worker was better. At least she listened. I told her my problems, but she told me that when my brother was adopted, his records were sealed. That meant I couldn't find out where he lived, much less visit him.

I couldn't cry. The tears wouldn't come. I had cried so much that I didn't have any tears left. I felt completely alone and helpless. I had tried so hard but I hadn't gotten anywhere. I didn't have anyone who understood me.

I ran home. My foster mother asked me what was wrong and I told her how they gave me the runaround. She got in touch with my law guardian, who is looking into this matter now.

I still feel my brother's adoption is my fault. I should have been there for David when he needed me and not pushed him away. I'm a blood relative, but I turned him away when he needed me most. I could have at least showed him I loved him.

Now he's in a complete stranger's home. I haven't seen him for three years. I don't know where he lives. I don't even know his new name.

And I didn't have a chance to say goodbye. The last time I saw him—in the playroom at our agency—I didn't know it would be the last time. I walked past him without saying anything, thinking I'd see him again the next day.

One of the last things he said to me was, "I hate Wunika," because I had told my social worker I didn't want to see him anymore. This was when I was sick of him, just before I knew he was going to be adopted.

I think of David every day—so much that it hurts. It hurts the most when his birthday passes. He's getting older without me.

I hope he hasn't forgotten me but remembers the times I took care of him as a mother. I don't want him to remember the times I rejected him.

I may have pushed him away when he wanted me, but that

doesn't meant I don't love him. The system didn't understand my history, my pain. They took away the only family I had. Now I don't have anyone to love.

I just hope it all works out and that I do get to see my brother one day.

❏

Wunika Hicks was 16 when she wrote "I Lost My Brother to Adoption" and, soon after, "She'll Always Be My Mother," the piece that follows. Born in Brooklyn, Wunika entered foster care at age 8 and spent the next ten years in the system, mostly with foster families. Writing about her experiences "opened up a lot of doors, because I had locked my feelings inside." In 1995, she enrolled as a freshman at the State University College at Brockport in upstate New York. She is also the author of two other essays in this volume, "Sista on the Run (From the Past)" and "A Vacation from Mr. Hope."

SHE'LL ALWAYS BE
MY MOTHER

Wunika Hicks

W hen I look back on my past, I wish I never remembered some of the things that happened to me. My mother was abused as a child, so in return she abused me.

I tried to be the best daughter for her. It just seemed as if she expected so much. I was only eight years old when I had to stay home from school to take care of my brother. When my brother was born, it seemed like that was when all my problems began.

One day my mother came home after a hard day of work. (Ha! Honestly, I don't know where she was.) She yelled at me as I was feeding my brother David: "Wunika, who the f-ck told you to give David that bottle?"

I didn't say anything, I just sat in the chair feeding my brother. I wished I could have disappeared. My mother yelled once again: "You're so damn stupid! Put David in the crib!"

I rushed to put my brother in the crib. I never envied my brother so much as at that moment. I wished I could have been in his place. My mother loved him so much. She once told me, "I wish I never gave birth to your stupid ass." Those words stick with me today.

As I walked back into the kitchen, my mother took the boiling pot of water off the stove (filled with bottles, tops, and nipples I was sterilizing) and threw it in my face. I never yelled so much.

My mother just stood there. She didn't care. All she said was,

"Shut the hell up." The skin on my face fell off. I yelled to the top of my lungs. My mother couldn't stand the noise, so she asked me: "Do you want me to give you something to cry for?"

I eventually stopped crying. My mother cleaned my face and boy, did I yell! She changed her attitude once she saw the damage she did. She apologized to me.

I never felt so much hate for her. I wanted her to hurt as I did.

When we went over to my relatives' house, all they could say when they saw my face was, "That's a damn shame." I suppose they felt sorry for me. They even bothered to ask my mother why she did that to me, but all my mother said was, "None of your f-ckin' business."

I felt so bad for my mother. I thought everything that went wrong was my fault. It seemed as if I couldn't do anything right. I couldn't do anything right at home and I messed up in school.

I felt as if no one cared for me. The teachers always wrote "IG-NORE" on the chalkboard because I was the class clown. I had no friends in school because I beat them up all the time. I hated everyone and I fought everything that moved.

One day in school I pulled a chair from under my classmate. The teacher came running. My classmate was crying because when she fell she hit her head on the chair. My teacher looked at me in disgust as she grabbed my arm and put me in my chair.

I went home with yet another letter in my notebook. I didn't have time to tear this one up. To tell you the truth, I forgot about it.

That night my mother opened my notebook to help me with my homework. As she turned the pages she found the letter. SMACK!—right across my face. I fell on the floor. I didn't bother to cry. I did bother to tell my mother that my teacher had grabbed my arm in class.

"WHAT? Who the f-ck does she think she is? No one puts their damn hands on my child but me! That white b-tch is really getting out of hand. Wait until I get up to that school, I'm gonna give her a taste of her own damn medicine!"

I was so tickled. I was happy that someone else was going to feel my pain.

The next day my mother took me to school. She busted into my classroom and asked the teacher why she put her hands on me. Boy, was that lady scared!

My mother didn't even give her a chance to speak. BAAM! My mother punched her right in the face. My teacher fell on the floor, the same way I fell so many times before. She was crying on the floor. I began to feel sorry for her. She just lay there, which was a good move because my mother was waiting for her.

Security came and grabbed my mother, and boy, was she putting up a fight. The teacher's mouth was bleeding. The children in the classroom watched in amazement. I remember one boy in my class saying, "You and your mother are crazy!"

My mother and I ended up in the principal's office. He told her that the teacher wasn't going to press charges. My mother really didn't care and she did a good job of showing it.

She ended up cursing out the principal. She even threatened to blow up the school and his house, too. I think he believed her from the way he ran to get Security. As Security escorted my mother and me out of the building, he told my mother not to bring me back. I'm sure you can imagine her response.

Our walk back home was a quiet one. As I stepped inside my room, I heard my mother say: "Take off your clothes!" I couldn't believe her.

Like any other child, I hesitated. I took my time because I didn't want the beating I was about to receive. My mother became impatient, so she grabbed me.

The only things I had on were my Garfield panties and my tights. There was nowhere to hide. I could hear the belt in my mother's hand say to me: "YOU AGAIN?"

I tried to run but my mother grabbed me by the ankles and beat me as she held me upside down in the air.

That night my mother wouldn't let me sleep with her. I had to sleep on the dining room chairs. We had mice, so I refused to sleep on the floor.

I woke up to David's yells. My mother was gone once again, and who knew when she'd return. I picked up my brother from the crib and opened the refrigerator. I took out his bottle and heated it up on the stove. He was still crying, and I felt like killing him.

I wanted to go outside with the kids from my projects, the Fort Greene projects. I got along with the children from around my way. The ones I hung out with all liked to fight.

I searched in the cabinets for David's cereal, to put in his bottle. As I fed him, I couldn't help but wonder if ma would someday beat him as she beat me. I doubted it. She gave him everything when she was around. He had more than I ever had, from attention right down to the clothes on his back! All I had to my name were one pair of pants and two shirts.

My family knew we were being abused, but they acted like they didn't see it. It was as if we didn't exist, as if we were nobodies. I wanted to hear someone say they loved me. I wanted my mother to say it to me and mean it, the same way she said it to my brother. But how could she claim to love me when she abused me every chance she got?

David sucked the bottle dry. I put him on my shoulder to burp him. Even though I was only seven, I already promised myself that I'd never have children. I had to admit, though, that I'd make a good damn mother.

Yuk! David threw up on my shoulder. I hated when he did that. I reached in the closet to get his tub. As I ran his water, David started making noises. I couldn't help but love him. He seemed to be the only one who was thankful for my services.

He loved me. He had to—I took care of him and he depended on me. I had to feed him, change his Pampers, and answer to all his needs. Even though I hated staying home, it was worth watching him.

David loved the water. He never cried when I washed him, but he'd yell when I took him out. As I dressed him and combed his hair, I wondered if our mother would be coming home that night.

I put David in his crib as I went to run my bath. He yelled at the top of his lungs. I promised him I'd be back soon. I rushed so he wouldn't cry for long.

As I washed up, it brought back so many memories. I remembered my mother leaving me at her girlfriend's house. David wasn't born yet, so I must have been six years old. I had to sleep in the same room as the lady's son, who was around sixteen.

That night he made me sleep in the bed with him. He made me touch his private parts. After that I couldn't remember anything, but I do remember crying to his mother and all she did was smack him.

My mother came to take me home. She told me to take off my clothes so she could wash me up. As she tried to wash my private parts, I'd yell. My mother asked me, *"What's wrong?"*

I was scared to tell her, I didn't want her to get angry. She asked her girlfriend, "What the f-ck did you do to my daughter?" The lady acted like she didn't know.

My mother picked up a chair and threw it at her. The lady started screaming. My mother went to get a knife and the lady finally told her.

That was the first time I saw my mother cry for me. She asked the lady where her son was, but he had left earlier that morning. My mother then beat the lady the same way she beat everyone else.

I remembered going to the hospital and the cops speaking to

me and my mother. In the end, my mother told me he was put in jail. It was as if I was bad luck to my mother, because everything I did seemed wrong.

David was still crying. I jumped out of the tub and flew to put on my clothes. As I ran to pick him up, I looked at him. He was so handsome, he looked just like my mother.

I felt sorry that he wouldn't grow up with a father. His father left my mother when he found out she was pregnant. He said he was married and couldn't take the chance of his wife finding out.

It was as if my mother had bad luck when it came to men. My own father died when I was two years old. My mother was never the same after he died. That's what my family said, anyway.

David looked at me as if he knew what I was thinking, because he cried even more. This time I cried, too. Why us? Look at all of them other children—they had a mother and a father. We had nothing.

I loved my mother to death but damn, give me a break! I wanted to live my life. Little did I know I'd be sorry when I got the chance.

My mother didn't come back home that night or the next. I cried so hard. I prayed nothing had happened to her. I didn't have any food, so I ate some of David's baby food (which wasn't that bad, by the way).

When my mother did return, she came with enough food to last the whole year. She acted as if she was gone for an hour. I wanted to question her, but I had to stay in my place.

"Where's David?"

I quickly said, "In the crib." I noticed her looking around the apartment. She asked me, "Did you let anyone in the house while I was gone?" Of course I said no.

My mother fixed my favorite dish, lamb in tomato sauce with rice. I wondered if she was okay. All I cared about was that she was home with me.

As I slept beside her that night, I felt so much safer. I just hoped it would stay that way, that I would always feel safe with her and not be scared. But something deep inside told me that the way we were living couldn't go on forever.

That hurt me. I didn't want my mother to go, just her attitude. I knew if she went away, I'd have nothing. She was a part of me and vice versa, regardless of all the bad things. She will *always* be my mother, I said to myself, just before I fell asleep.

MY CREW
WAS MY FAMILY

Craig Jaffe

I ran away on the day my adoptive mother found out I had stolen $1,200 from her. I had stolen the money over a period of six months, but by the time she found out I had already spent it all. I knew I had to run away because she was about to go off on me.

When she put me on the back porch (like she always did, whenever she got mad at me) and went to call the cops, I had my opportunity. I grabbed a shirt off the clothesline and a pair of socks. Then I picked up a pair of rubber duckies (rain shoes) and jumped over my next-door neighbor's fence.

At first I didn't know where I was going. Then I decided to go to the movies like I always did when I ran away. I had no money, so I snuck in through a side door. I saw *Robin Hood: Prince of Thieves* and then left.

It was five P.M. by that time and I was getting hungry, so I decided to go to Key Food and help the people with their bags. I stayed for two hours. I would have stayed longer, but I knew I had to keep moving. From what, I had no idea.

My first night in the streets was horrible. I slept in the bushes by the church, down the block from where my mother lived. I couldn't sleep that well because I had to keep one eye open to make sure that nobody saw me.

For the first three weeks in the streets it was the same thing over and over. Sneaking in the movies, then bagging groceries to make money, then going to sleep with one eye open.

After the third week I knew I had to move somewhere else because things were getting too quiet. I thought about the beach. Since it was the summer, it would be hard for people to find me in a place that was crowded during the day and dark as hell at night.

The first couple of days at the beach were very good. During the day I would help the fishermen by running to get coffee and donuts for them. At night I would go on the piers and watch people catch crabs. Whenever I got tired, I would sleep under the boardwalk.

I stayed at the beach for two weeks. Then I left because I thought I saw my mother there one day.

My next home was in a bunch of bushes in the projects on Nostrand Avenue. It was a good place to hide because they were very bushy and it was impossible for anybody to see me.

Once I crawled inside, I was concealed from the rest of the world. I never got wet when it rained because I put an old shower curtain on top of the bushes and wore my rubber duckies and raincoat. The only real problem I had was when the ground became muddy. Then I would wind up in Waldbaum's bathroom, washing myself longer than usual.

After a while my lifestyle got boring. I wanted to try something new. It was my life now and I could do anything I wanted to. So I decided to try cigarettes.

When I bought my first pack I was mad scared. I didn't know what the hell I was doing. My hands were shaking when I gave the guy the money. Then he handed over my first pack of Marlboros.

When I took my first pull I thought I was going to die. I started to cough and choke on the smoke. I dropped that cigarette so damn fast that I burned myself.

After I stopped coughing I took out another stog and lit it up. This time I didn't inhale, I just took a pull and let it stay in my mouth for two seconds and then blew it out.

One day when I was bagging groceries at Key Food, this girl came up to me with her friend and asked me if I had $1.25 so she could buy a forty. To be honest with you, I didn't know what the hell a forty was, but I told her to come back in fifteen minutes because I didn't have the money. She said okay and left.

Fifteen minutes later she came back by herself. She asked me if I had the money. I said yeah and gave it to her, then she left. About twenty minutes later she came back and asked me if I wanted to come and chill with her for a while. I said yeah.

When we left the store, she started to ask me questions about where I lived and what my name was. I gave her my real name but a fake address. She told me her name was Lisa, but that her crew called her Dimples. Then she asked me if I wanted to hang out with her crew. Not knowing any better, I said yeah.

We walked to the corner and sat down. After two minutes of silence, a whole bunch of guys came from the opposite corner. They came toward us with a somewhat arrogant walk. They got closer to us and I started to get nervous. When they got two feet away from us the skinniest one said:

"Dimples, what's up?"

"Nothing, what's up with y'all?"

"We chilling. Who's the kid?"

When he said that I looked away, scared of what might happen.

"He cool, he cool."

That made me turn my head back.

"Whatcha mean?" said a guy with a bald head.

"Exactly what I mean. He cool!"

"So you saying Shorty going to be down with us?" another guy said, who looked half-white and half-Puerto Rican.

"Yeah."

Someone from behind the crowd yelled, "Ah sh-t, Shorty down with the crew!"

"Yes, Shorty!" someone else screamed.

Then they all came towards me and I stood up. One by one they gave me a pound and told me their tags.

"Whuz up, I'm Sprite."

"Photo."

"NWAP." (Which stood for N-gga with a Problem.)

"Guess Man."

"Yeah, whuz up, I'm Smiley."

About fifteen of them told me their tags. It was a mixed posse, whites, blacks, and Puerto Ricans. I thought I was so cool. I thought that I was finally going to be who I really wanted to be. But little did I know what that was.

Life was a breeze for me. There was no one to tell me what to do or where to go. I was running with a gang and doing my thing. Sometimes I would wonder what my adoptive mother was doing back home. Was she crying, laughing, dying, or surviving?

All of a sudden I'd stop and remember that she was the reason I was in the streets. When I lived at home, she would physically abuse me and treat me differently from her biological children. Now I didn't need her or her family because I had my crew. My crew was my family.

When I first became part of the crew, I didn't know anything about drinking beer or smoking buddah. The thing that I did know was how to survive on my own.

My first blunt came to me as a surprise. I had no idea that my crew would actually give me one. At first I didn't know how to smoke it, but then they taught me.

"Here, Shorty."

"What's this?"

"A blunt."

"Oh, sh-t."

"What?"

"Nothing, it's just that I ain't never smoked one before."

"You for real?"

"Hell, yeah."

"Okay, this is between me and you only."

"Yeah."

"You hold it and take a pull like this."

He took the blunt from me, then put it to his lips and took a long pull. He held the smoke for about ten seconds, then let it out.

"So that's how you do it!"

"Yup, ain't nothing to it. Here, you try."

I took the blunt and did the same thing he did—took a pull, held it in for ten seconds, and then let it out. The smoke burned my throat and I started coughing.

"Easy, Shorty, easy."

"Damn, what the hell you trying to do? Kill me?"

"If you weren't going so damn fast, maybe you wouldn't have f-cking coughed."

"Fast? Then why don't you show me how f-cking fast or slow to go?"

"Here, now watch me very closely."

He took the blunt from me and did the same thing he had done before. Then he handed it back to me.

"You see, you got to have finesse. Don't rush, but don't take your time. You'll get the hang of it. Here, try again."

I took the blunt from him and took another pull. Not too fast, not too slow. When I finished blowing out the smoke I handed it back to him. This time I didn't cough or choke. Although it burned my throat, I didn't show it.

"You see, now you got the hang of it."

He gave me a pound and we both finished off the rest of the blunt. Once in a while I coughed, but then I would stop immediately.

By the time we finished I thought I was in a different world. When I stood up I broke out laughing. I don't know why, but I did. I kept laughing for a half hour. Then I had to stop because my stomach started to hurt me. The only thing that Mark did was just sit there looking as stupid as he was.

When I had my first bit of weed is when things began to change for me. I finally had a chance to escape and go on my own little adventure. Whenever things got bad for me, all I did was gather up some money to buy a fat Phillie and my problems were gone.

Or at least I thought they were.

Day after day I hung out with my crew. When they went home, I went to make some money. By the time we met again I usually had about ten dollars on me. That would be enough to buy two nickel bags or a dime bag.

The sorrow I felt for my adoptive mother and family was no longer present. A feeling of hatred took its place.

After the weed came the beer. If I drank a forty and smoked a blunt afterwards, I would be f-cked up! I would do that almost every day. I was becoming an alcoholic and a drug addict and I was only thirteen years old!

Things were fine for a while until I went back to my original hobby. Stealing. To be honest with you, I used to love stealing. It was the main thing I was good at.

I used to steal anything from clothes to food. Sometimes me and the crew would go out together and bumrush stores. Since I was the smallest but quickest one, I usually came out with the most stuff. Stealing was the main way that I got clothes when I was on the street.

When my crew began to notice that I was a near-expert at stealing, they decided to show me how to steal something bigger and much more valuable. Never in my wildest dreams had I thought about stealing a car.

That night when we got ready to leave, I thought about not going. But Guess Man talked me into it. On the way, they gave me a few pointers.

"When you're popping the steering column, try to cut down on the noise."

"Since you are the lookout person, whenever you see somebody coming, knock on the car once and walk away, then come back in five minutes. Got it?"

"Yeah, got it."

"Okay, let's do it!"

We walked for about forty-five minutes until Photo stopped in front of a Lincoln Town Car.

"This is the one we want. Right, NWAP?"

"Hell, yeah!"

"Let's get to work."

Photo and NWAP got in the car. Mark, Smiley, and me stood by the car, while Sprite and Reggie waited on the corners. They wanted to make sure that the cops wouldn't pull up on us.

Then we started. I glimpsed into the car and saw NWAP and Photo trying to pop the steering column. After about three minutes of noise they got the car started.

Photo rolled down the window and told us to hop in. I was so scared I was shivering. Me, Mark, and Smiley hopped into the back seat. We went to the corner and got Sprite and Reggie, and off we went to steal another one.

After we stole our second car of the night we went to a big field across from Marine Park and played Crash-a-Derby. The way you play it is by crashing the cars while you're driving around in a circle. After we finished, the car doors were smashed in, the front hood was part of the windshield, and they were stuck together like Siamese twins (kids, please don't try this at home).

We finished our fun at about three o'clock in the morning, and unfortunately we had to walk back. Afterwards we went to the store and bought cigarettes and beer. We chilled until about six A.M., then we split up and went our separate ways.

As I was walking back to my hiding place in the bushes, I started to think about life and why my life had turned out the way it was. I knew it was my mother's fault, but it wasn't fun being a criminal. That was the only thing I was experienced in doing. Stealing, drinking, and smoking were three of my favorite things on the streets. I was just another problem that society couldn't handle. I knew I had to change my lifestyle, but I didn't know where or how to begin.

The summer was coming to an end and my crew had to get ready to go back to school. Most of them had gotten left back the year before, so this year they had to do good or else their moms would kick them out of the house.

There were times that they used to ask me what school I was going to. I would tell them that I wasn't sure yet and immediately change the subject.

When school did start, my peeps had mad new clothes. I wanted new clothes too, but new clothes don't last when you're on the run. On the run from the truth—the truth that I had made my life the way it was and I was the only one who could change it.

Day after day I would watch my friends go to school and get an education. The only thing I was doing was making money for weed and beer.

On Saturday my crew and I would stay out late, but on Sunday nights the crew had to go in early because they had to go to school. When they went in I would stay out later, just hoping the 5–0's wouldn't catch me.

Every day I got more and more depressed. I needed someone to show me the right way. I needed someone to care for me and to love me. I needed someone to tell me who I really was.

Three weeks after school started my crew was chilling on a Sunday night. It was still early, 9:30 P.M. Then for some strange reason they kept on asking me when was I going to go home. I kept telling them that I couldn't, because my mother wasn't home yet.

By 10:30 Lisa and Photo said they would walk me home. They said it in such a way that I couldn't use the excuse, "My mother isn't home," anymore. So I said peace to the rest of the crew and we began walking.

"So, Shorty, what does your mom do?" Photo asked.

"She's a nurse."

"Really!" Lisa asked, sounding surprised.

"Yeah, really," I said.

We made a left turn onto the block where I told them I lived, although I really didn't. I was starting to get nervous.

"Do you think she's home now?" Photo asked, looking down the dark block, then turning to me.

"Nah."

"Is anybody home?" Lisa then asked while lighting up a cigarette.

Oh, sh-t! I thought to myself, *I think that they know. What do I do? Do I run? Nah, can't do that, 'cause Photo with his Speedy Gonzalez ass would probably catch me.*

"Huh?" Lisa asked again, breaking into my thoughts.

"Nah, nah, nobody home," I said.

We kept walking down the block until I stopped at a house with a white iron fence and no car in front. I told Lisa and Photo to go wait down the block until I waved, because I didn't want my neighbors to tell my mother that they saw me coming home with a bunch of kids.

They walked down the block and stopped. I turned towards the front door and pretended to knock on it. Then I stepped inside the doorway and waved, but then instead of them walking away they walked towards me. When they got about ten feet away, they began to talk.

"Craig, we know about it," Lisa said.

"Know about what?" I said, walking closer to them.

"You know," Photo said.

The jig was up. They knew about it, but I tried to play it off.

"Know what?" I asked again, trying to sound more serious.

"Know that you ran away from home," Lisa said, lighting up another cigarette. It began to drizzle.

"But how do y'all know?" I asked again, almost crying, but trying not to.

"Sprite—"

"Sprite what?" I asked, cutting off Photo.

"Sprite followed you home the night that you and him went out to steal cars. He saw you go in the bushes in the projects on Nostrand Avenue," Lisa said.

"Damn it, damn it, damn it," I said. It was finally over. My dream life had come to an end.

"I also knew," Photo said, and we started to walk again.

"And how did you know?" I asked, sounding like a smart ass.

"I knew because I did the same thing you did when I was your age!" he said, almost yelling.

Then Lisa said, "You wanna talk about it?"

We walked towards the park and sat down on the table. There was no longer a drizzle. I began talking.

"I ran away from my house three months ago because I had stolen twelve hundred dollars from my adoptive mother. I've been living on the streets. For money I've been working in Key Food. You know, helping people with their bags and stuff like that. Please don't turn me in!"

"We have no choice," Lisa said. "Sprite talked to a guy he knows who is becoming a cop. The cop said that we would have to turn you in, or else we would get arrested."

That was it. I couldn't let my crew get arrested, so I let them turn me in. They called up the rest of the crew and we met at the police station. When they took me in, the cop at the front desk said that there was no record of me being missing, but they took me anyway.

The first thing the cops did was ask me a whole bunch of questions, such as "How long were you on the streets?" and "Where does your mother live?" and "Why did you run away?" Then he gave me some donuts with an orange soda. I asked him if I could see my friends.

He said that I could, but not to go far because a police car was coming to pick me up to take me to a shelter. I walked out of his office and back into the waiting room. Nobody in the crew was talking.

"I guess this is goodbye," I said, trying to put on a smile.

They all got up and one by one they gave me a pound, along with some advice.

"Yo, Shorty, take care of yourself," Photo said, while handing me two twenty-dollar bills. I put the money in my pocket and gave him a pound.

"Shorty, I'm going to miss you. Don't forget to call us," Mark said, while handing me a piece of paper with everyone's number on it.

"Don't f-ck up. You don't want to end up six feet deep," NWAP said.

When it was Lisa's turn, she didn't give me a pound or advice. She gave me something I had always wanted—a nice long hug. A hug that I always will remember.

Then a tall black cop came in and told me it was time to go. I gave everybody one last pound and walked outside. A cop held the door open for me.

When I got in the cop car, I looked out the window. Lisa and the crew had their heads down. Both cops got into the car and slammed the doors behind them. I looked out again. Their heads were up. As the car slowly pulled away, I put up the peace sign and turned ahead.

It took an hour to get to the shelter. But in that one hour I thought about my life. I knew I had to change it.

I had already learned the first step. I had to stop running. It wasn't my mother or my problems that I was running from. It was myself.

After I went into the shelter, I was placed in the system. Now I'm in a group home and I've turned my life around. I have no contact with my adoptive family due to the fact that I refuse to go back and live with them. But I lost all contact with my crew, because I lost their numbers when I was in the shelter.

I dedicate this story to my crew, who understood somebody I didn't know—Me. I haven't forgot y'all. Peace.

❏

Craig Jaffe, 15, was born in Bogotá, Colombia, and was adopted as an infant by a family in Brooklyn. Family problems led to his running away from home and entering foster care in 1992. Initially placed in special education, he eventually entered mainstream classes and excelled academically. Active in school and community affairs throughout high school, he was awarded a United Federation of Teachers' scholarship to attend college. He now goes by his birth name, José Reyes.

SHORT TAKES: REMEMBERING FAMILY

I'M GRATEFUL TO MY MOTHER
Ishan Grant, *16, Queens, N.Y.*

I'll always be grateful to my mother for helping me through tough times. She was always there for me, until one day it all came to an end. BCW came and as quickly as I knew it, we were gone. They took us away and put us in a foster care place. If you are wondering who we are, it's my older sister, my little brother, and my niece.

I hate reliving that harsh moment, but I have to express myself this way in order to let it all out. When they put me in a group home, it all started coming back to me, as if I was going through it again.

Everybody is here for a reason, and my reason is that I got too much stress. But I know why I'm here and I'm trying to make the best of it by going to school and doing what I have to do. It's hard being young and on your own. I always wanted to be on my own, but it's not as easy as I thought it would be. Now I know that I need my mother more than ever. This group home does have some effect on you, because it makes me see that I have to be more responsible to get what I want in life, and my goal is to get my family back together again.

THE KEY TO HER HEART

Peggy Roedeshimer, *16, Santee, Cal.*

I can't exactly remember the last day with my family. My parents got a divorce when I was eleven and I have been in and out of the system since I was nearly an infant.

Yet I do remember that each time I left my home to a new foster family, there was a cold and empty feeling inside me. I always cried with a lump in my throat and nauseous butterflies in my stomach.

After the divorce, they put me back at home with my mother. My two sisters remained in foster care. As I lived with my mother we were always fighting and arguing. I hung around the wrong group of friends and began shoplifting and smoking pot.

I had to be the adult sometimes and take care of my mother because she has schizophrenia. I wanted so badly for me and mom to get along, but she just didn't have the power to help me. And I wasn't willing to get help.

One hot day in September I was out on the playground when the principal walked up to me and wanted to take me to the office with her. I only thought I was in trouble again, but once she opened her office door and I saw two social workers sitting at a desk, I began crying.

I begged the social workers to give me one more try, but there were two police officers to escort me home to get my belongings.

I ran upstairs, opened the door, and fell into my mother's arms, telling her how sorry I was and that I had to leave again. We both cried as we packed my clothes in an old suitcase, and carried it to the police car. I remember neighbors watching me. They all were shaking their heads at me. I felt scared, afraid, lonely, and disappointed in myself all at once. Me and my mother cried and hugged, and she gave me a necklace with a key on it. My mom told me the key was to her heart. I then got in the police car and they drove me away screaming.

I now have grown and learned from the system. I miss and love my family. My mom calls me three times a week and I see her a couple times a month. I only live twenty minutes from her.

As I go on seventeen, I have realized that everything has happened for a reason.

STILL WISHING

Larita Bishop, *16, Oklahoma City, Okla.*

The last time I was with my real mom was when I was four years old. I can remember me and my two sisters were crying because we didn't want to see our mommy go to jail. I can remember my mom was outside fighting with the police for some reason. I remember we were looking out the window watching everything and eating hot dogs.

I remember this tall white woman pushing past my mother and the police coming towards our front door. Phyllis, being the oldest (five), said we should hide somewhere. Me and Misha followed Phyllis to the front closet and hid inside.

Somehow that woman got us out of the closet. She never once yelled at us, she was really nice. She picked Misha up and told us to follow her. She led us outside to the police. She began talking, but I don't know what they were saying. They put all three of us in a cop car and took us to the Kentucky Shelter.

That was the worst thing that ever happened to us, because we loved our mommy, but in a way it turned out kind of good because we were placed with our grandmother in Lawton, Oklahoma. We also found out we had other sisters. I wish we could see our mother again and start all over.

Phyllis told me she wishes our mom could be there for her high school graduation, but her wish won't be coming true because next fall she'll be in the twelfth grade. I still have three years left for my wish.

MY FATHER WASN'T THERE

Kareem Powell, *18, Port Washington, N.Y.*

My mother tried her best with me. She raised me with love and spoke wisdom into my ear, including all the clichés that mothers tell their kids, like "Don't talk with your mouth full," "Always say please and thank you," and last, but not least, "Everyone makes mistakes."

Everything was almost perfect at home except for the absence of a father whose visits I can count on one hand. No letter, no phone calls, not even twenty-five cents for a postcard sending birthday wishes. All I ever heard of him was disheartening news, but without his testimony I was forced to believe it. I was too young to comprehend what was going on, but seven-year-olds aren't supposed to understand grown people's problems.

When he was there I should have latched onto him until he knocked me off. Maybe he would have felt pity and could have been able to talk about what made him so angry and why he left. Was it me or the responsibility that he couldn't handle? I regret feeling the hate that made me put his memory in the farthest, darkest corner of my mind. His support could have saved me from the lust for money, that propelled me to sell drugs and buy clothes just to look like everyone else. I ended up in the system and I guess it was for the better. I don't know him anymore, so we might as well be dead to each other.

I wish I could see him to know whether he's dead or alive, but it's been eleven years since I was seven, and since then he's not seen his son. There are handfuls of mistakes that everyone makes and it is a shame that we only get one ticket on the merry-go-round of life. Ironically, everyone wants to erase the past but few want to change the future. A future filled with pain, if one man's mistake continues to be another man's regret.

Fathers, love your kids!

SEARCHING FOR A FATHER
Laura White, *19, Bronx, N.Y.*

I am nineteen and have never met my biological father. When I was growing up I lived with my mom, my sisters and brother, and a man named John who I thought was my father. But at age ten, I found out that John was actually my stepfather.

On that day in the fourth grade I was called down to the principal's office. He asked me why I was using two last names on my papers. I told him those were my names and he didn't ask me anything more, but as I walked back to class I was confused.

Later that day I went home and told my mom, and that's when she explained to me that one of the names was from my biological father. John was the father of my sisters, but not of me and my brother.

That hurt, because why did I have to find out through school? Maybe if I had been told in another way I wouldn't have been so humiliated.

I still loved my stepfather after I found out, but when I was twelve my mom and John separated. When they separated, the pain of not knowing my biological father really hit me. I felt I had to find out who he was.

But for a few years I didn't do anything about it. I had no idea how to go about finding him. Then one day when I was sixteen I started my search. I looked all through the phone book to try to find his number, but a lot of people had the same first and last name as he did.

Then one day I found not only his first and last name but his middle name, too. I called the number and a woman answered.

I explained to her that I was looking for my father and that her husband had the same names he did. She did not sound upset at all. She was very nice over the phone. She told me it could be possible but that he was not home, so I left my number with her.

Later that day he called me back. He asked me many questions. He asked me if I had a brother with his first name. I said yes. He asked me what my name was. I told him Laura White. He also asked me my mom's maiden name. So I told him.

I felt very scared answering him, because why was he asking me all these questions? It seemed like as soon as he heard my mom's maiden name, he got a little excited and said, "I'm sorry, but I'm not your father."

Today I still wonder if that could have been my father and he was just too afraid to face the truth.

About two weeks after the phone call I was sitting on the subway and a man was standing right across from me. I kept staring at him because he fit the description of my father that my mom had given me. So I went over to him and said, "Excuse me, sir, but what is your name?"

This guy was looking at me like I was crazy. Sort of like, *What is this young girl doing?* But he did tell me his name and then I said, "I'm sorry to bother you, but I thought you could be my dad."

He didn't say anything else and neither did I, but his expression showed that he thought I was sick and I felt kind of embarrassed. Then my stop came and I got off.

Whenever I ask my mom about my father, she says you only have one father and that's the one who raised you. I respect and love my stepfather for doing that and I always will, but I still feel there's a part of my life that's missing because I never met the man who made me and I guess I never will. Maybe there is just no hope for me. I could be standing right next to my father and not even know it.

Sometimes I question whether my mom is really telling me the truth when she says she doesn't know where my father is. She could just be saying that because she's angry at what she went through with him. If so, that's not fair to me.

That's where a lot of parents go wrong. That's why I am hurting today. Right now my father is probably in his own little world, not even thinking about me. I am the one left wondering where he is and if I will ever be able to find him.

To all fathers: although you may not be ready, your child needs to know who you are. You should have thought about your responsibilities in the heat of the moment, because you made the child who needs you today. No one says you have to be involved with the mother, because the child is what is most important. If things can work out, it would be better for both of you to bring up your child together, but if not, you can at least let your child know who you are because every child needs a father.

II
LIVING IN THE SYSTEM

THE RESIDENT'S CREED

I'm gonna succeed
I'm gonna make it
You may not believe me
but I'm young and strong
and I'm moving on
to make a place for me

So shake your head
and think your thoughts
as if I am deceived
but the last horse in line
doesn't always finish last
by chance it takes a lead

You notice my wrongs
and when I fall off the track
but you never take the time
to give credit that's due
when I dust off my knees
and start back

I have many more laps to go
and, yes, bleed blood if I must
bleed because I know
somewhere, out there, there's a
finish line, my destination

whatever it is,
whatever it is,
I will reach it
I will succeed,
you will see

—Tameka Ross, 19

MY DAY IN THE GROUP HOME

Carlford Wadley

My day starts with the staff members turning on the lights and shouting, *"My man, time to get up!"* A few minutes later I roll out of bed, having heard them shout for the hundredth time. But when the staff gets tired of waking us up the "nice way" (after their lungs or our eardrums have given way), they get nasty.

Nasty is pulling off our covers, pushing us out of bed, or a particularly rude kind of awakening which they gave to one kid. Here I will change all names to protect the innocent (and the not-so-innocent).

Well, there was once this kid named Peter (his real name is . . . uh-huh, like I would really tell you that his actual name is Dave). The staff always had problems waking him up. So one day Dave—I mean Peter—turned around in his bed and saw something that shocked him. It was long and smooth. It was inches from his face. It was a . . . a live snake. (If you were thinking what I thought, you have a very DIRTY mind.) All that could be heard was a loud scream and a heavy thud as Dave fell out of bed.

Anyway, let me get back to the subject. After we get out of bed we use the bathrooms. I try to get in there quickly because after certain residents have used the bathroom, it looks like they have not only cleaned themselves but a pig as well. The floor is wet and dirty and a few of my fellow residents seem to have forgotten that toilets can be flushed. Oh Lord, the smell could knock you out.

"My man, time for breakfast!"

We finish brushing our teeth and head for the breakfast table. I always love going into the dining room. The furnishings, provided with love by the State of New York, are superb (NOT!). Especially the bookshelf, which is decorated with books and makes it seem like the kids in the group home actually read (that's a good one).

Depending upon who is on duty, we get either a decent breakfast or something that tastes like a rubber tire. When we have a good one, it is usually eggs, accompanied by toast, English muffins, and other tasty tidbits.

However, when we get a bad breakfast we can usually blame one particular staff member (I don't mean to instigate anything, but D*****, you're not such a bad cook, it's just that everyone else is so much better!). Then we usually have cold cereal or tasteless hot cereal which takes a mountain of sugar to stomach (YUM-YUM!).

"My man, time for chores!"

Chores range from mopping the floors to cleaning the bathroom. It is bothersome to have to tell the rest of the loitering kids to get out of my way so I can do mine. After chores we leave the house to go to school, where one madness replaces another.

Back home I miss study hour as usual, so I go and watch some TV. The group home TV is a total wreck. It looks like something you would get suckered into buying at Insane Arnie's. The buttons are pushed in to the point of no return and the remote doesn't work.

But so what—who really wants to watch a show about a white housesitter who babysits three mutants and has a friend who makes Bubbles the Ape look like a brain surgeon?

Time to do laundry. Using the washing machine is always an adventure in fear because you never know what it will do. The contraption has been known to damage clothes and to magically change their colors.

If that isn't bad enough, I have to time the machine manually since the cycle is stuck at rinse. Halfway through my wash I hear them calling us.

"My man, get your #@$ up here for dinner!"

Dinner shows how the most normal activity can be turned into an episode from the Twilight Zone, especially if the person cooking can burn coffee. We might have chicken or perhaps instead we'll have chicken (just kidding—we get other types of food, it just seems that we have chicken 90 percent of the time). We recite the same tired, musty prayer that the Flintstones' great-grandparents probably said and then we finally eat.

While we are eating the conversation drifts to the subject of a former resident, Dewayne. He was the most thieving %&$#@! I ever met. He would steal everything that wasn't nailed down and even then there was no guarantee.

I remember once I was making a sandwich in the kitchen and I went out for a moment to talk to the staff. When I came back I found that my sandwich was gone and that the little thief had locked himself in the bathroom where he was chowing down. Dewayne's stealing eventually got him promoted: Spofford.

Someone at the table mentions that when he saw Dewayne recently, he was living phat with dope gear and a mouthful of gold caps. I'm thinking to myself that Dewayne was probably trying to hurry up and sneak away before his old friend noticed that his Cross Color jeans and gold caps were missing.

After we eat we go to do more chores. I love cleaning the kitchen because I'm able to go in the fridge and "borrow" some extras. Then I go to check on my laundry and dry it.

"My man, get your %$#&$ ready for bed!"

By this time of the day I am so tired of hearing "My man" in every sentence. Tomorrow I might go on a day pass, but I have no wish to compete with the enormous line at the phone tonight.

I retire to my room where my roommate's feet knock me out and give me an unpleasant dream—I am still in the group home at age ninety-nine (goddamn!), Dewayne is now stealing gold-capped dentures on the down low, and "My man" is shouting at me to hurry up in my wheelchair and get my @&%$# to school . . .

❏

Carlford Wadley, 16, was born in Jamaica, West Indies, and grew up in Brooklyn. He entered foster care at age 14 in 1991 and has lived in group homes in the Bronx and Manhattan. Carlford has worked at Scholastic Inc. as an intern, plans to study literature and journalism in college, and wants to be a writer. He recently published an opinion piece about foster care budget cuts in Newsday.

FINDING A FATHER
IN THE SYSTEM

Clarissa Venable

H ello, my name is Mr. Dugue. What's yours?"
I looked at him and hated him already. It was my
first day in the group home and Mr. Dugue was one of the staff members. I hated him because he was a man. I couldn't stand men after what they did to me in my family.

I was adopted when I was seventeen days old and my mother was already fifty-two. She adored me because I was her last adopted child and the baby in the family.

My three adopted brothers were much older than me. When I was young my mother used to spoil me and her sons didn't see anything wrong with that, but as I got older things started to change.

My brothers had been used to getting all the attention, but now that my mother seemed more distant with them, they didn't like it one bit. By the time I was nine years old, I was getting abused emotionally and physically by my brothers.

When they came home, they would come straight to my room. I used to be so scared. I'd hear them come in and pretend that I was asleep. Then they would come and shake me and start the abuse. My mother never knew what was going on. For all she knew we were a happy family.

I started to fall apart. I used to be a straight-A student, but now I could barely maintain a C average. I used to be outgoing, but now

I didn't give a damn about anyone and was always starting fights. I took out all my anger on the person I was fighting.

One day when I came home my brother James started punching me like I was his worst enemy, and busted my lip, both of my eyes, and knocked up my ear. He was high on crack. (Up 'til this day, I can't hear well out of that ear.)

That night I put ice on my face and tried my best to get the swelling down. I didn't go to sleep because I was scared. In the morning, my mother thought I had a fight on the street. I wanted so bad to tell her that it was James, but I didn't have enough courage.

The next day I went to court. I was in shock when my lawyer just came out and said, "She's being abused." The judge said, "For now, she's going to a group home."

I said 'bye to my mother. She was crying. I was real scared about going to a group home.

The van came to take me away. I said to myself, *No more men to look at.* And for the first time in a long time, I smiled.

I was shaken awake by my caseworker and she told me we were there.

I looked up and saw a big house. It was blue and white. I got out of the van and walked to the house.

My caseworker rang the bell and a pleasant-looking woman came to the door and said, "Hi, my name is Ms. Jordon." I said "Hi" and went inside.

The place was furnished well for a group home. I expected it to be like a shelter because of the name, Sheltering Arms. And even though I had never been to a shelter, I knew they weren't nice.

I was led to the back office and gave them my name, my age, and other information. I was so happy not to be with my family that all I did was smile through everything. I was thinking, *No more men!* I was real happy to be in a house that was all girls.

I was sitting there smiling when I heard a deep voice. I was thinking, *Damn, what kinda lady has a voice like that?* I got ready to greet the lady when all of a sudden a man came in, saying, "Hi, my name is Mr. Dugue. What's yours?"

I instantly started crying. I was so hurt.

With all my problems with my adopted brothers, how could they put me in a group home with a man?

The first thing I asked was, "Are there any more men?" Ms. Jordon said there were not. I just said to myself, *I'll stay away from him.*

The next day was good. The girls in the group home were nice. I had a best friend in there named Carlean. She showed me that there will always be good friends.

Since she was being nice to me, I let go. Like I said before, I didn't care about anyone, but she was so nice to me that I thought, *I guess there's nothing wrong with having a best friend.*

Carlean and Mr. Dugue were talking one day when I went in the office. He said hi. I said hi and left. It surprised me that he was nice to me. No man ever said hi to me, really seeming like he meant it.

But during the next couple of days I found out that he was so sweet and so nice that I had to like him.

Whenever Mr. Dugue saw me upstairs by myself, he would come over and talk to me. Whenever he saw that I was sad because I was thinking about my mother, he would make me laugh. He would say something out of the blue that you weren't even thinking of.

Like I would be in my room, or in the living room reading, or watching television, when Mr. Dugue would fly in the room and jump in front of me. Then he would fly back out of the room.

We also would play our special game. Mr. Dugue would swear that I passed gas. Then he would take the Lysol can and spray the room.

Mr. Dugue showed me that not all men are the way my brothers were, even though it took me a while to believe that.

I started really trusting him one night when we were talking and playing around. When it was time for me to go to bed, I told Mr. Dugue goodnight. He said, "Goodnight, daughter."

That really touched my heart. I never had any male tell me that I was his daughter. I also thought that I would never see the day when one did. So when Mr. Dugue said that, I knew that I had the father I never had before.

When I got to know people on the block and started breaking curfew, he taught me that it was okay to have friends, but it wasn't okay to break curfew. He told me that if I kept breaking curfew, I was going to get in trouble and eventually get discharged.

One time I had a problem with an old boyfriend who lived around the corner. Mr. Dugue told me not to talk to the guys around there. He explained that the boys around the area were no good. They were all in a gang, and it wouldn't be good to get involved with them.

He taught me that school came first before anything. He said that there's no future if there's no school. After he told me that, I went to school again and had a lot of friends.

He made my self-esteem go back up. I really started caring about myself and others.

The only thing I regret now is not being at Sheltering Arms anymore. I had a problem in the group home, so they moved me. But I still got all the lessons down pat that Mr. Dugue taught me.

❏

Clarissa Venable, 16, has lived in several group homes in the Bronx and Brooklyn. One thing Clarissa wants to change about the foster care system is the cycle of anger between residents and staff. "What I would like to do is get staff who understand the troubles we are going through, who will look at the bright side of things, and who are willing to help us emotionally." Clarissa recently earned her high school equivalency diploma and plans to attend college.

SISTA ON THE RUN
(FROM THE PAST)

Wunika Hicks

I was getting ready to cook one Friday night when I asked my foster mother, Ms. Roberts, a question about dinner. She didn't hear me and asked me to repeat myself, but when I did she still didn't hear me. It seemed like I had to repeat my question twenty times before my foster mother finally heard what I said.

I was very annoyed, and as I walked out of her room I said, in a sensible tone, "Man, you act as if I'm speaking an alien language."

(Would you believe she didn't hear that, either?)

Ms. Roberts's daughter heard what I said and told her mother, and then Ms. Roberts called out after me, "Wunika, what did you say?"

I guess she wanted to see if I'd say the same thing again, so I walked back into her room and repeated myself. When I did, Ms. Roberts slapped me right across the face.

The moment she slapped me I went racing for the front door. Ms. Roberts yelled after me, "Wunika, come back, come back!" but I didn't look back. I ran right into the street and kept running until I ran out of breath. I just wanted to disappear.

I ran out of the house so fast I didn't have my jacket. It was raining, but not even that could make me turn around. I wanted to call my friends in the Bronx or Queens. I wanted to get the hell out of Brooklyn. But I had no money or my phone book, so I sat down on the sidewalk in the rain to think of my next move.

I couldn't believe Ms. Roberts slapped me. Is that how adults express themselves when something goes wrong? (And they say *we* don't act our age.)

A couple of houses down from where I was sitting was a house that looked very familiar. It was my friend Nate's house. What drew me to the house was that I remembered speaking on the phone to Nate's mother, Mrs. White. She's very special to me.

I had talked to Mrs. White for the first time on the phone about two weeks before. She was so interested in me and asked me so many questions. She was happy I was friends with Nate and said I would be a good influence on him because she liked my attitude.

I never had that kind of conversation with an adult before. Most times when I talk with an adult, it never seems real, but Mrs. White was so open and honest. I'd never met a lady so warm-hearted, someone who honestly cared about *me*.

I got up off the sidewalk, rang the doorbell, and Nate's brother Chris greeted me inside with a smile. I asked him, "Is Mrs. White home?"

Chris took me to his mother and Mrs. White welcomed me with open arms, saying, "So you're Wunika!" (It was the first time we actually met face to face.) I was able to crack a smile because this lady lifted my spirits completely.

I told her I had run away from home because my mother slapped me. I didn't say "foster mother." It seemed so difficult to tell Mrs. White I was in foster care. I didn't want her to think I was a "troubled child."

She looked at me and said, "Your mother hasn't ever hit you before?"

Then I told her it was my foster mother who hit me, and Mrs. White shook her head as if she immediately understood.

She said she realized I didn't think I had done anything wrong. On the other hand, Mrs. White could also understand where my foster mother was coming from. Ms. Roberts may have been under stress, she said, and couldn't handle me talking to her in that way. I just listened to Mrs. White explain what a mother goes through.

I tried to look at both sides of the story, but I still felt my foster mother was wrong. Ms. Roberts felt that I spoke to her disrespectfully, as if she was one of my friends, but even if I had, did that make it right for her to slap me?

Ms. Roberts doesn't know that she sometimes makes me feel like my biological mother used to make me feel—like I can't do anything right.

My biological mother used to beat me for no reason, just because she was angry. She told me to keep the bruises on my body a secret from everyone, but if she was in a good mood she'd be very nice to me and say, "I'll be there for you."

My mother hurt me and made me not trust her. How can you claim to love someone and then hurt them every chance you get—physically and mentally?

My foster mother doesn't know about my past. She doesn't know that everything I once owned has been taken away from me.

My brother has been adopted and I haven't seen him in years. Perhaps he wouldn't have been adopted if I could have shown him I loved him.

My mother abused me and I take some of the blame. I just wish I could have been a better child.

My relatives didn't take me into their home when my mother couldn't take care of me. Maybe if I wasn't such a "terror," they would have accepted me.

Even my virginity has been taken away. I was raped by an older boy when I was six.

This is a past my foster mother doesn't know. She doesn't know that I feel as if I have nothing. She doesn't know I have been abused. Perhaps if Ms. Roberts knew my past, she wouldn't have slapped me. When she did, it was like my mother slapping me all over again.

My foster mother is a decent person. I have more things than many foster children. Yet I still feel as if something is missing. There's an empty spot, a void somewhere.

I've lived with Ms. Roberts for four years now, and she has never asked me about my past. She says, "You can always come to talk to me," but a child has to truly feel that, and for me it's not there.

I feel divided. I want her to know my past, but I don't want her to judge it, to say "how terrible" it was. I don't want her to ignore it, but I don't want any extra attention. I don't want to feel awkward and I don't want anyone feeling sorry for me.

And I don't want people giving me advice when they haven't been through what I have. They're just on the outside, looking in. I want to understand myself first before I let someone else try.

Perhaps I will someday find help from someone who has been through what I've been through and who's found the answers. But until then I need to do this on my own. I was the one who suffered alone. Let me recover that way, too.

Mrs. White phoned Ms. Roberts because she didn't want her to worry. When Ms. Roberts came to pick me up, Mrs. White explained my feelings of anger. My foster mother explained that I'm the child and she's the adult, and that I should speak to her with respect. She felt I had disrespected her.

I thought what Ms. Roberts was saying was one-sided, but I didn't want to say anything because I knew it wouldn't be polite. So I just kept quiet and ignored her.

When it was time to leave I gave Mrs. White a big hug as the tears just came rolling down my face. I didn't want to let go, I just wanted to stay attached to her forever. We did finally part.

I'll never forget what she told me as we were about to leave: "Wunika, I'm going to be your second mother." Those words felt so good. I melted all over.

I need that mother figure—that is the void in my life. I didn't have a bond with my biological mother, I didn't have one with my first foster mother, and I don't have one now with my second foster mother.

Don't get me wrong—I believe in God. He has done a lot of things for me and I promise to always praise Him. But I need that earthly mother and I'm just lucky I've found her.

Not much has changed in my foster home since the night Ms. Roberts slapped me, but ever since our "little incident" she seems to know my limits and vice versa. I will remember what she told me: "Wunika, you can't say everything that comes to mind."

But I also want to be able to express my feelings. My biological mother never let me do that. She would say, "A child should stay in a child's place." I can't remember ever having a decent conversation with my mother—I was too scared she'd think I was coming out of that "place."

Nothing will ever change the way I feel about my past. It's a part of my life, it affects me every day, and it will never be forgotten. You can never run away from the past. I will eventually grow stronger from it, but it has already given me strength right now.

Since the night my foster mother slapped me, I speak out to her when things aren't going right. I'm in touch with how I feel, with how I should be treated.

If anyone takes advantage of me, if anyone talks to me or treats me unfairly, I will let that person know, regardless of who they are. I will say what I have to say with respect. I will watch what I say and how I say it. But it will be said.

❏

Wunika Hicks wrote "Sista on the Run (From the Past)" when she was 17. It is the third in a four-part series of pieces in this book exploring her childhood, her relations with her birth and foster mothers, and her life in foster care.

WHY I'M BETTER OFF IN FOSTER CARE

Angela Rutman

G oing into foster care was a nightmare come true. My mother had always made it my worst fear. She told me horrible things about it, and I was more scared to be separated from her than anything in the world.

The first time I went into foster care I was eight years old. My mother and I were living in a homeless shelter at the time. She wasn't taking care of me right, so I went into a foster home. A few months passed, then my father got out of jail. He found out that I was in a foster home and began to visit me.

I was so happy that I didn't care about my father's drug addictions. I also completely blocked out the fact that he had molested me when I was seven years old. All I saw was my chance to get out of foster care and to have a real family.

It took a while, but the CWA finally let me go back to live with my father and his new wife. My father tried to force a mother-daughter relationship on us too fast. It ended up causing friction. He also began molesting me again. I felt dirty and I hated myself. I began to hate the rest of the world for all of my problems.

My father signed me into a mental hospital when I was fourteen. I was put in the teenage ward because I was depressed and not going to school.

The night before I went to the hospital, my father told me not to tell anyone that he had sexually abused me. I really wanted to believe that the abuse wasn't making me miserable, although it was. It's sad that my father brainwashed me into saying what he wanted me to say and feeling what he wanted me to feel.

Being in the hospital was safe and relaxing. It was unlike anything I ever felt before.

I got up enough nerve to tell my roommate what my dad was doing to me, but I made her promise not to tell anyone. My roommate told me to tell my therapist, but I wouldn't listen.

I began to feel depressed again, because I knew that I would have to go back home in a couple of weeks.

Every day in the hospital we had community meetings for everyone on the floor. We discussed our problems and told the rest of the group what was going on in our lives. You could say anything you wanted to say in the community meetings.

One girl began to talk about her brother sexually abusing her. I knew if I talked about my situation, I would be safe. I wouldn't have to worry about my father coming after me. I didn't care about him abandoning me either, because now I had people on my side who were stronger than he was.

At one community meeting I got up enough courage to come out with the abuse. At first I didn't think I'd be able to do it.

My arms and chest went heavy when the staff asked if anyone had something else to say. I couldn't raise my hand or open my mouth to speak. My body went numb.

Somehow I managed to raise my hand. When I was called on and before I could speak, I broke down and cried. I had never really cried about the abuse before. I threw the words out from my chest, crying hysterically like a baby.

It was the hardest thing I have ever had to do, but it changed my life. I decided not to even try to work things out at home. I agreed to be put into residential treatment.

Being away from my family made my whole life easier. I still had the depression and self-hatred, but at least I now had staff and therapists who would listen to me.

I was given chores and a bedtime. For the first time I ate meals at a table with other people. At home I always ate dinner alone, which was usually something that I could pop in the microwave, because my parents were never there.

Whenever I needed someone to talk to, staff were there most of the time.

For the first time I was being listened to, without getting hit if someone didn't agree with me. When I lived with my parents, they were too busy telling me their problems. They thought that I shouldn't have problems because I was just a kid.

I adjusted to the rules well, because I liked the way the rules made me feel safe. I never had any structure in my life before. Foster care gave me a lot of structure, which is what I needed.

Now, a lot of times I feel like breaking the rules because I've had a lot of structure for the last year. Sometimes it feels like the staff enjoy putting me on restriction or taking money from my allowance. It's like they get off on controlling my life. I have to admit that this is how I feel when I don't get my way.

But I know that the staff are enforcing the rules because they care. Sometimes they'll take out their own problems on you. Some just haven't got the training to know how to deal with us. But in my group home, that doesn't seem to be a problem.

I'm not gonna lecture you about how you should respect staff and follow all the rules. I just feel that foster care can be a good experience for some kids. The rules are designed to protect you and give you structure. If you have a problem following those rules, it's probably because you weren't getting enough structure at home.

If I didn't go into foster care, I would still be back home, living miserably with my parents. I would be much worse off because I wouldn't have dealt with my problems. I would be praying for my father to have an overdose, because back then that was the only way I saw out of my pain.

I'm much happier living in foster care. Even if I had the chance, I would never go back home to my family. The group home I'm in now is my real home.

❑

Angela Rutman, 16, grew up in the Bronx and Manhattan and now lives in a group home in Westchester County, N.Y. She volunteers as a religious instruction teacher with first graders. Angela plans to major in English in college and wants to be a teacher.

CAN THE COUNSELORS
KEEP A SECRET?

Anonymous

Have you ever confided in a staff counselor about your past life, your dreams, or your secrets? When you ask her to keep it confidential, of course she says, "Don't worry. This is between you and me."

But are the counselors really keeping it confidential? That's something we all have to wonder about.

I often suspect that the staff counselors are talking about the kids among themselves after the chief administrators go home. Evening, night, and weekend shifts seem to be the best times for them to go into their offices for their private, "important" meetings.

Ha! Sounds more like Happy Hour to me!

When I was in a residential treatment center in Westchester County, I never told a staff counselor about my problems. And when I moved to a group home in Manhattan in December '92, I still didn't have faith in counselors—until about a month after I moved in.

My social worker wasn't in the residence that day and I felt depressed. There was no one to talk to because my friends were still at school or work, but I needed to talk with someone. So I decided to give this "trust thing" a try.

I told a staff counselor why I was gloomy. I told her not to repeat my story to anybody, not even to the other counselors. She said, "Don't worry. We'll keep it confidential."

Later on that evening, the staff had their usual private meeting in their office. Somehow, I felt paranoid. I remembered when I first came to the group home, the kids told me that certain staff counselors gossip about the residents.

When all the counselors got together for their meeting, I waited for a few seconds and then tiptoed down the hall, bent down, and pressed my ear to the door.

Sure enough, I heard my name a couple of times. Then I heard them calling me "a b-tch," "a dirty stinking bum that doesn't know how to take care of herself," and a "brat who acts like a little baby and is difficult to handle." The "trustworthy" staff member told the other staff parts of the story I told her (she misinterpreted some of what I said) and then they laughed and made fun of me.

You could imagine how I felt—angry, hurt, dumb, and regretful that I even said "hi" to the staff! I wanted to kill them all and then spit on their graves!

To this day, the only time I talk to the staff is when I ask for carfare to go to school or work, or when I have to do my laundry.

It's sad to know that if you trust some staff counselors, the next day they gossip about you like a dog. It's almost like telling your friend a secret, and then she stabs you in the back.

If I have anything I need to confide or get off my chest, I talk to my therapist at our sessions. Or if my therapist leaves for the day, I talk to my close friends and tell them whatever's on my mind.

So it's not like you don't have any choice but to talk to a staff member when you feel sad and depressed. You can talk to your therapist or to your best friend.

Or maybe there's a staff counselor who you absolutely trust, who doesn't gossip about your secrets during the staff's Happy Hour.

❏

Anonymous wrote this story when she was 17. The fear that personal matters are not kept confidential by group home staff is common among foster care youth.

MAKING
A NEW FAMILY

Lorraine Fonseca

I hear a lot of kids say they wish they were back home instead of in the group home, or that they can't wait 'til the day that they can finally leave foster care. But that's not what I say or feel.

Believe it or not, I like living in foster care. Not just because I get clothing money, allowances, stipends, and social workers and guidance counselors hooking me up with school or a job, but also because the friends that I live with have become my family.

Before I even knew what "foster care" meant, I had a "dilapidated" family. Back then, my father was an alcoholic and a diabetic. He died in '85.

My mother and I were at opposites after she met her boyfriend. We were constantly arguing and fighting. I was also at opposites with my uncle and grandmother. They would take sides against me. They were never wrong and always 100 percent correct.

My aunt and cousins? Well, since I haven't heard from them since Madonna's very first single, "Everybody," came out, I guess I don't have any aunts or cousins.

And then there was my school nightmare. I'd like to tell you how it changed my attitude, my self-esteem, and my personality (and why it made me cherish my friends so greatly).

The school nightmare began when I was in fourth grade. I was a quiet and shy girl. A boy named Lester Morales started by calling me "Germs." Then about five boys started calling me names.

By the end of two months, the whole class played the cooties game. I could've been a good sport and played along, but it wasn't really a game. From then through sixth grade, I was the "cooties" girl. I had a few friends, but unfortunately, I kinda lost contact with them.

I thought things would be different when I graduated from elementary school to junior high, but it was worse. When the kids from my new class tried to get to know me, I was scared and stayed away. That whole semester, they didn't bother to say a word to me. I acted like that because I was afraid that the bad experience I had in the past year would happen again. And it did. The same boys had also transferred to my junior high.

Boy, did they embarrass the crap out of me by still playing that cooties game! My grades were good, but slipped a little. I was depressed every day because of that. I had a school counselor, Mr. C, and he was great (I miss him!), but this problem was getting out of hand and I didn't feel any better.

Graduating from junior high was nothing for me to feel great about. I couldn't say farewell to friends or miss them or shed tears because I was a loner. I had shed enough tears already from the beginning of the school year and I was just relieved it was all over.

The reason why the same boys kinda "followed" me to junior high was because they lived around my way. Some of them lived (and still live) in the same building as me. It got to the point that I had fights almost every day with them. I was beaten up badly, but I didn't care.

One Sunday, a boy (who looked more like a bodyguard) kicked me in the leg just because I said "Shut the hell up" after he dissed me.

At the beginning of the new school year I had to go to Jane Addams High School for the simple fact that I wasn't going to even try going to James Monroe with the same kids.

One night I was alone outside in the park crying. I had pen and paper and drew stick figures committing suicide. I tried to figure out why those boys treated me the way they did. My thoughts were like this:

They weren't joking with me.

It's not a cooties game. Games like that stop by the time you go to seventh grade.

They really hate me.

But I swear I never bothered them, said anything, or went near them.

I don't look like a creature.
So what's the problem?
Why do I feel like I can't go near my mother when I need help?
Why do I feel like I don't have a mother?

By then, I thought about the other problems with my bio family, etc. I went home and went straight to the bathroom. I popped pills in my mouth and then felt like I was going to die. I almost did.

So to start off the new year ('87), I stayed in the hospital for a couple of months. Though I begged to go home, I'm glad I didn't. The hospital wasn't all that in the beginning because some girls acted hardcore (or psycho).

But during my stay, I made friends. People who love you and care about you and look out for you and *understand* you and don't betray, backstab, change on you, or hit you. You'd call them friends. But since I'm a sensitive soul, I call them family.

I left the hospital and went to an RTF (residential treatment facility) in Westchester County in '88.

I was in an apartment with eleven girls. At first, some of the girls didn't like me. They thought I was conceited. I rolled my eyes at two girls named Rosa and Marianna, then smiled at them. That was to show them that I wanted to be their friend. It was strange, but that was my way of communicating since my socialization skills hadn't blossomed yet.

One day, the girls asked what my name was.

"Lala," I said.

"Well, Lala, why do you keep rolling your eyes at us?" they asked.

I said that I was only joking with them.

"But we don't even know you," they said.

"Well, I guess I'm a little scared to say hi and say my name," I said.

"Well, there's no need to be scared, we ain't gonna bite you."

I laughed a little because I didn't know what to say.

"Well, I'm Rosa and this is my friend Marianna."

And from there, we were friends.

Weeks later, Marianna started calling me and Rosa her two daughters. Their boyfriends were my "daddies." It was a little family game we played.

I've always felt Marianna was like a mother because she acted like one. She always wanted me and Rosa to hang with her. She made sure nobody messed with us. She'd always be there to listen.

Like one time, when I came back from a home visit crying. I

couldn't deal with my bio mother any longer. She had the kids from the neighborhood who called me the "cooties" girl chilling in her house. I felt kinda betrayed. It's like she was saying to me: "Well, who cares if they bothered you or hit you? That's not my problem."

Well, Rosa and Marianna demanded to know what was wrong and I told them what happened during my home visit. They hugged me and said, "Don't worry about that. You're with us now."

God, you don't know how great I felt to hear that! We all went outside to meet our friends from the other apartments after dinner. The guys made us laugh with their usual antics.

We always chilled and parlayed together. At school, even if we didn't have the same classes, we chilled outside between classes. During the first three months in the RTF, I made new friends and my family grew.

We were always together through good times and bad. Trips, parties, school, detention at the gym barn—we were always together. Obviously that's because we lived together, but we were more like a family than just a group. And even though there were some kids I didn't like, I had fun at my RTF.

We talked with each other about our problems with staff, like why certain staff think they're all that just 'cause they live at home and we live in an RTF.

We talked about what happened in our lives and how our families treated us. I was shocked to hear that some of my friends' stories were worse than mine.

But even though we were very close, I never thought that they would look out for me.

One day a girl from another RTF confronted me about some rumor that was spread about her. (You see, her RTF and my RTF didn't mix. It had been that way even before I came to the RTF. I don't know why. But whenever they heard a bad rumor, they'd blame it on one of us, even if we didn't say a damn thing about them.)

She started with the usual, "Were you talking about me a few minutes ago?"

I had an obvious answer. "No, why would I say something about you if I don't even know you?"

"Well, my friend said you was talking about me, and my friend wouldn't lie and . . ."

My friends saw what was going on and they were there to have my back. They told her to leave me alone or they would $%# the girl up.

I was shocked. I was like, "Oh damn! They stood up for me?"

I was at a loss for words. (Honest!) Why? Because I never had people stand up for me before.

One night, when it was lights-out at my RTF, I did a lot of thinking. I decided not to go on any more home visits or contact my bio mother. I was sick and tired of trying to work things out with her and the rest of my bio family and having it go nowhere. It just got me more upset.

When I moved to a new group home in '92, I was very upset that I had to leave my family at the RTF (I gave them all a hug and cried.)

But I continued to make friends and expand the family in my new place. Only this time, I didn't have any "mommies," "daddies," "aunties," etc. (Unfortunately, those days were gone.) Just good, loyal friends.

I think the key to living better in foster care is to have a positive attitude and outlook, and to know what good you can gain out of the system. I don't pay attention to staff bossing me around. I don't pay attention to staff who give me detention for little things like being five minutes late or missing level meetings (at my first RTF I cared, because I wanted to go on trips).

Actually, I think it's fun to argue with staff (in a good-natured way).

My gain was new friends and learning a lot from them. I learned more from my friends than from my whole bio family put together. I learned the Golden Rule. I am loyal, respectful, and kind to others who treat me the same way.

❏

Lorraine Fonseca, 17, had been living in foster care for six years when she wrote this story in 1993. She has said of her writing, "I hope I can bring a perspective to other kids in foster care from my point of view . . . to let them know they are not alone."

WHY ARE YOU DOING THIS, MR. JONES?

Anonymous

A fter having my baby at the age of seventeen, I had no place to call my own. So I had no choice but to go into a mother-infant program. (It's a group home, but the only thing different is that you live there with your child.)

When I entered the mother-infant home with my child, I was scared and nervous. I had never been in foster care before, but as the minutes went by I became more relaxed because of a staff member who made me feel right at home, and in my heart I felt that I could trust him.

The first week at the mother-infant program went pretty good. Ms. Days helped me take care of my newborn baby, while Mr. Jones, my social worker, helped me try to figure out what I wanted to do with my life.

I knew right then and there that I didn't make a mistake by having a baby, because with the help of the staff I could continue with my schoolwork as I raised my child.

My second week at the group home was even more comfortable. I felt nothing could go wrong. There were times that I would look at my daughter and tell myself how much she looked like my mother.

After I put my daughter to sleep, I found myself thinking about the fun things me and my mother used to do together. I never understood the real reason why she threw me out of the house, and at that point I really didn't care.

I missed my mother so much that I was crying at night and very depressed. So I had to find a way to see her, because a year and two months without contact is a long time, and she didn't even know that I had a baby.

I told my social worker, Mr. Jones, about crying at night and how it was making me so depressed. I also told him that I needed to see my mother, because she was the main reason why I was crying. He automatically asked me for my mother's address and phone number.

Then he told not to worry, because he was going to try his best to get in touch with my mother, and I was pleased with that.

Two days passed, the worst two days of my life. I didn't hear from Mr. Jones. I wondered if he got in contact with my mother. I wondered how she would react when Mr. Jones told her that I had a baby. And then I had to deal with the baby crying. I was going through hell.

After the third day, I finally received a phone call at night from Mr. Jones, telling me that he called my mother. She was not home, he said, but he left a message.

I was mad that it took him three days to give me that message. I told him thanks for calling and was about to hang up, when Mr. Jones asked me what I was doing. I told him I was feeding the baby and then, after that, I was going to give her a bath.

Then Mr. Jones asked me if I was going to be at my house tomorrow. I told him, "Yeah, why?" He said, "Because I'm supposed to check out the house and make sure that everything is okay and I really want you to be there."

I told him sure, no problem, and I hung up the phone and continued to do what I was doing, until my mother struck my mind again and I found myself crying.

Around twelve P.M. the next day Mr. Jones came to the house. I was still in bed. Ms. Days came in my room and told me that Mr. Jones wanted to see me and the baby. So I got up, went into the bathroom, washed my face and brushed my teeth, and went into the living room where Mr. Jones was waiting.

He asked me where the baby was. I told him that she was asleep and I didn't want to wake her up because she had a hard time falling asleep.

Mr. Jones and Ms. Days started talking, then all of a sudden it was quiet. As I went into the kitchen to get something to drink, I felt Mr. Jones staring at me hard. I tried to pay it no mind, because I was still upset about the message he gave me the night before about my mother.

Mr. Jones didn't leave the house until something after one P.M. I was glad when he left. I went downstairs to check the mailbox, because I was expecting a letter from my baby's father, who was in jail at the time.

I received three letters—two from my baby's father, and the other one was from someone who wrote on the outside, "Open it up and look what's inside."

I thought the letter was from my baby's father but I was wrong. It was from Mr. Jones. Now I knew there was something wrong.

Later that night I received a phone call from Mr. Jones. He told me that he had gotten in touch with my mother, and that she was kind of upset that I had had a baby and that she needed time to think about seeing me.

I was so happy to hear that Mr. Jones got in touch with her, but I was also afraid to ask him why he had written me a letter that said he found me attractive. I told him thanks and hung up the phone.

I thought hanging up would give Mr. Jones a message, but it didn't.

On July 8, 1992, Ms. Days went on vacation and another staff came to take her place. Around twelve P.M. I received a phone call from Mr. Jones. He told me that my mother wanted me to come see her and he asked me if I felt comfortable if he came and picked me up.

Like an a--hole, I told him yes. I guess he was excited, and he told me to meet him at the train station.

He finally came and picked me up at around one P.M. I was mad because he kept me waiting for a long time, but in a way I didn't give a sh-t because I was on my way to see my mother and she was going to see her first grandchild.

As we drove in the car, I could feel Mr. Jones looking at me hard, real hard, but for some reason I wasn't scared.

After coming off the bridge we were in the Bronx, instead of Manhattan where my mother lived. I asked Mr. Jones why we were in the Bronx. His reply was, "Because I live in the Bronx and I need to change my clothes before I go into Manhattan."

I didn't ask him why he needed to change his clothes, and I left it at that.

He stopped in front of a blue building and got out of the car. He told me that he didn't think that I should wait in the car for him because the neighborhood was really bad, so I agreed to go upstairs with him.

When we arrived in Mr. Jones's apartment, I went into the living room while he went into his bedroom. He asked me if I wanted anything to drink. I told him no, and then he started to talk about the carpet in his bedroom. He suggested I come and see it, so I laid my baby down on the couch and went into his bedroom to see what he was talking about.

All of a sudden Mr. Jones started hugging me and telling me that I felt and smelled good. I told him to get off me and tried to force him away from me, but he wouldn't let me go.

I was screaming and yelling, thinking that somebody would hear me and come knocking on the door to see what was wrong, but nobody came. My baby didn't even wake up from my yells.

Mr. Jones forced me down on the bed and told me to shut up. He told me that he wanted some from me. I told him no, and asked him why was he doing this to me.

"You're supposed to be my social worker, you're supposed to help me, not try to have sex with me!"

His reply was, "It's after five P.M. and I'm not nobody's social worker now."

Then I said, "If you don't get off of me, I'm going to tell the people at the agency."

As Mr. Jones looked at me, he had my hands gripped tight to the bed. He started kissing my breast and my neck and said, "Those people at the agency don't care about you. I'm your social worker and they ain't going to believe you."

After hearing that sh-t I was really mad now. I really wanted this man off me, so I started kicking and tossing around but it didn't work.

Mr. Jones continued to tell me about how the people at the agency don't care about me and my baby. I didn't believe him, until he started talking about one of the staff members in the house who used to hit on a girl and scream at her.

When the girl told the agency, they said that they would look into it, and when they did, Mr. Jones said that they believed the staff over the girl. He also told me that everything has to go through him, he's the one who has to call my mother to see if it's okay for me to come home on weekends.

"So who's going to believe," Mr. Jones said, "that I had sex with you?"

After hearing this I started to think, *Why is the agency like this? Why do they treat us wrong?*

I also was thinking if I was to have sex with Mr. Jones, he would let me go on my weekend pass anytime, and I could come back to the house anytime I wanted, and Mr. Jones wouldn't say anything to me because we had done something together.

While I was still thinking about what to do, Mr. Jones started kissing my breast, then the kissing started to get heavier, and then he started to play with my legs. I wanted to scream, but I also wanted to go on a weekend pass with my mother. I was confused and didn't know what to do.

As soon as Mr. Jones asked me if he could have some, I told him yes. I figured one time wouldn't hurt. I would just pretend that I wasn't there.

After he was finished, I was ready to go home. I felt sick and dirty.

When Mr. Jones dropped me off by the train station in Queens, he told me that he would see me the next day and that I would definitely get to see my mother. I told him yeah, whatever, and walked away. I thought that night would be the first and last time that I would have sex with Mr. Jones, but it turned out that I was wrong.

After the first time I had sex with Mr. Jones, we continued to have intercourse for about two months. During those two months, Mr. Jones had me thinking that the agency didn't care about me and that he was the only one that I could trust, and I kept believing this for a while.

But one day me and Mr. Jones had intercourse unprotected and he came inside me, and a couple of days after that accident I asked Mr. Jones, "Suppose I am pregnant? What should I do?" And his reply was, "Well, if you are pregnant, it ain't from me because I know I'm not the only one that's having sex with you."

After hearing that, I finally realized that Mr. Jones was using me and abusing me mentally.

He was my social worker. I had to ask him if I could stay outside late or if I could leave my baby with my aunt, and whenever I asked him, Mr. Jones said he would think about it. And when he said that, I automatically knew what that meant. It meant that I had to have sex with him in order to get permission.

The last thing that made me realize that Mr. Jones was using me was when he told me that he would help me and my mother unite again, but he never did. I was the one who called my mother to see how she was doing. The only thing Mr. Jones did was call her and tell her that I had a baby and that I was with his agency.

And when I finally saw my mother, I asked Mr. Jones if I could spend the night at her house, being that I hadn't seen her for a long time. Mr. Jones said he'd think about it, and for me to meet him down-stairs so he could talk to me, but I knew what that really meant. I told him okay, but I never went to meet him.

That following Monday Mr. Jones was upset with me and put me on restriction for two weeks. He said the only way that I could go outside is if I came to his house. I was mad because I knew he put me on restriction for that one time I didn't meet him downstairs.

I told myself that I had to stop having sex with Mr. Jones be-cause I hated the fact that every time I wanted to do something, he was always telling me he'd think about it, and then said he wanted to have sex with me. He never told the other residents that. He either told them yes or no right off to whatever they asked.

So I finally stopped having sex with him and had to deal with restriction for a while.

I called my mother to see how she was doing. She asked me why I didn't come and see her that much, and I told her that I really didn't feel like traveling all the way from Queens to the Bronx. I guess she understood because she never asked me anymore.

I knew deep down in my heart I couldn't tell my mother about the abuse from Mr. Jones because I knew that she'd be very hurt.

The abuse from Mr. Jones made me not trust anymore. I didn't tell anybody that I had sex with Mr. Jones because, like he said, who would believe me over him?

But six months after the abuse began I was ripping up inside, both mentally and physically. I couldn't help but share my experience with somebody, so I told my counselor at high school what happened to me. I knew that I was in the wrong for letting Mr. Jones have sex with me, but I needed to tell somebody how I was feeling.

I thought my counselor would put me down and tell me how much I was in the wrong, but I was mistaken.

Instead, she told me, "It's not your fault because he's supposed to help you. You were raped because he made you do something that you didn't want to do. And not only were you raped, but you were abused mentally."

I was feeling really good because I finally had somebody on my side. Mr. Jones told me that nobody would ever believe me, but I guess he was wrong for the first time.

My counselor told me that she strongly felt that I should tell the people at my agency. "Mr. Jones should not get away with this," she said, "because if he did it to you, he could do it to someone else, and it might be even worse."

I was feeling bad now because I didn't want everybody to know my business, but in a way I knew he did rape and abuse me, and that's something that I couldn't forget, so I agreed that I would tell on him. I wanted Mr. Jones to be put in jail. I agreed to tell my story, but only if my counselor was going to stick with me and she agreed.

After my counselor set up an appointment for me to tell the agency, I was kinda nervous, but I had to do what I had to do, because I have a daughter and I didn't want the same thing happening to her.

On the day of my appointment I couldn't help but cry. I told Sam, the head social worker at my agency, everything that was going on between me and Mr. Jones. I told Sam that I felt ashamed and embarrassed. Sam told me that I had no reason to feel that way. "If anybody should be ashamed and embarrassed," he said, "it should be Mr. Jones."

Sam told me not to worry because he would report it to the State. He told me that it would take a while for the paperwork to be done, and he asked me if I would like to see a counselor to talk about it. I told him no, because I wanted the counselor from school to see me every week. He agreed and everything was set.

Two weeks after reporting Mr. Jones to Sam, I had an appointment to meet with a lawyer in Manhattan. My counselor came with me to make sure that everything went all right.

As soon as we arrived at the courthouse in Manhattan I was happy, because I knew that the lawyer would be on my side and she would help me put Mr. Jones away. So I didn't have any fear in my heart.

A lady called my name and asked me and my counselor to come into her room, and as we entered the room, she asked me why I was there.

The lawyer started asking me questions and then she asked me to repeat my story to her, and as I repeated the story I found myself crying because it was like I was going through the abuse and the suffering all over again.

After finishing my story, I could feel that the lawyer felt sorry for me and I knew that she was going to help me put Mr. Jones in jail.

Finally the lawyer spoke and said, "I can imagine what you are going through and I want to help you the best way that I can, but your story isn't a case that can be handled, because you gave it up to him without him even having to take it from you. And when somebody takes something from you and you say 'No' and they take it anyway, then that's what you call rape, but in your case you were just used."

I told the lawyer that Mr. Jones had forced me down on his bed to have sex, but she said there was nothing she could do.

I was mad and upset and told the lawyer that Mr. Jones was right when he said, "Ain't nobody going to listen to you." Then I started to cry and kept asking myself, *Why did it have to be me?* My counselor couldn't help but rub my back, and she thanked the lawyer for trying to help me.

My counselor walked me downstairs and asked me if I would be all right. I told her yeah, knowing damn well the sh-t was eating me up alive, knowing that Mr. Jones was out free and didn't give a damn how he hurt and abused a girl twenty-seven years younger than himself.

My counselor told me that we still had to go to the State. They were the ones who could really determine whether or not Mr. Jones should be punished. I was so mad and upset that I didn't even respond to my counselor.

Three weeks after my appointment with the lawyer, I had another appointment with the State. While they were asking me questions I felt relaxed, because every time I stopped or paused they said, "It's okay, I can understand what you might be going through, take your time, it's all right."

And after I finished my story one of them said, "No matter what, you should not feel ashamed of yourself, because what he did to you was wrong, and as soon as we go back to the office we are going to get started on this case."

After hearing that I was glad but also sad, because Mr. Jones had been recently fired from the agency not because of what he did to me, but for other reasons. Still, I was beginning to feel more relaxed because I finally had the law on my side.

After two months the State asked to see me again. I was hoping to hear good news, but all they did was ask me if I could tell my story over again and describe what Mr. Jones's house looked like. And when I finished, there was nothing but silence. I told myself they probably wanted to see if I was lying to them, but that wasn't what it was.

They told me that when they interviewed Mr. Jones, he denied everything and told them that I was lying. And the only reason why they asked me to describe the house was because that could be something they could use against him. They also told me that they would get in touch with me to tell me what happened.

It's been nineteen months since the last time that I talked with the State, and I haven't heard anything yet. I think they probably dropped the case, or else I would have heard something by now. Maybe they didn't have enough evidence or maybe they didn't know who to believe.

They probably have forgotten all about me, like Mr. Jones said they would. He was right—they don't even care about me and my baby, and I guess that's why he's still a free man. He can find a job anywhere and just forget about the job he was fired from.

But as a teenager and as a mother I can't forget, because my past will always be by my side, no matter how hard I try to forget about it.

It's always going to be a part of me, and, as I watch my daughter grow up, I'm very confused. It's like she's getting more beautiful each day, and as a mother I can't help but think about how it's going to be for her when she gets older.

I know she's going to have lots of boyfriends, and one day she might have a male friend who she trusts, and I ask myself, *Will she know the difference between rape and sex? How should I explain the difference to her? Should I tell her what happened to me?*

A Message to the Readers:

Writing this story was very painful, but in the long run it has made me a stronger person. It has made me sure about myself. So sure that I can still trust other people after having an experience like this, and, by the same token, feel that what happened to me was not my fault.

Rape is never the fault of the person who is raped. It took me a long time to understand that Mr. Jones raped me and that it was not my fault, but now I don't blame myself and I am a stronger person for it.

The message that I would like to send off to you is this: if something bad has happened to you or anybody that you know, try not to let it put you down. Let it be an experience that will make you even stronger than before. And one more thing—never feel that you're alone. Other people may have had a similar experience and can understand you.

I realize that I'm not alone in this situation. At first it was hard to talk about it, but experiences like yours and mine happen every day.

❑

*Anonymous wrote this account in five weeks during the sum-
mer of 1993, when she was 18. She was inspired to tell her story
after reading another young writer's article about having been
abused. She is now out of foster care, has her own apartment,
and is working and attending college, where she is studying to
be an accountant. She says, "My relationship with my mother
is now very good, and the one thing I really learned is that the
key to success is communication."*

HOW I BECAME
A STRONGER MOTHER

Anzula B. Richardson

T here I was back in placement, but this time it was different—I was pregnant. Rosalie Hall in the Bronx was a strange place. They told my mother it was a maternity residence, but to me that was just a fancy name for a group home for pregnant girls.

I was two months pregnant and I would have to spend my entire pregnancy there. I wanted to be back in Georgia with my boyfriend Lorenzo. We were supposed to go through the pregnancy together. What would become of our relationship? Would we be a real family?

All kinds of questions were running freely in my mind. So many different feelings were jumbled up inside. I couldn't gather them all together, or even begin to sort them out. I knew that the social worker couldn't do that for me, either.

But thanks to the Mentor's Program at Rosalie Hall, I was able to begin to gather and sort out all my questions and feelings. They pulled me under their wing in the third month of my pregnancy. They began to help me face the decision I had made to keep my baby.

I can still remember Mr. Parker, the assistant director of Rosalie Hall, telling me that I was referred to the program because he thought I could benefit from it. I usually ask a lot of questions when I hear about something new, but for some reason I didn't care to know too much.

Mr. Parker explained that the Mentor's Program was organized about three years ago to prevent teen pregnancy by having pregnant and parenting teens go out into the community and share their experiences by speaking in front of groups of young people.

"And this is what you want me to do?" I said. "Well, sure . . . I guess so." I can remember not really caring.

Peggy and Catrina, both teen mothers, were going to train and counsel me. They were supposed to help me write out what I wanted to share with the kids at a local girls' club. I was really nervous, not so much about speaking in front of people as about sharing my story.

That's when I realized I was scared to death of becoming a mother. But I also was sure my boyfriend was going to be there for the baby and me. I wasn't worried about finishing school, because my boyfriend had graduated and he had a good job. Why did *I* have to get a job?

Boy, did I have a lot to learn.

After hearing stories from other girls in the Mentor's Program, I had to check myself. One of the girls went through her entire pregnancy with her baby's father, but after the baby was born he no longer wanted the responsibility. Another girl was left by her baby's father as soon as she told him she was pregnant. After hearing these stories, I had to re-evaluate my relationship with Lorenzo.

Was I living in some fantasy world? Was having this baby the wrong decision? Some of the things one girl said about her baby's father sounded just like Lorenzo. Her baby's father was supportive of anything she did and was always right by her side. He did whatever he could for her—just like Lorenzo.

But would Lorenzo really be there for me?

Damn, I went into the program with a lot of questions, and now I had even more.

My fifth month of pregnancy came around and I was snapped back into reality. Lorenzo had started to change. He didn't call or write as much as he did when I first left. When I would call him in Georgia he wasn't home, and his mother told me he was hanging out. This was taking a great toll on me.

But because some of the girls in the Mentor's Program had warned me, I was prepared to deal with it. They taught me that it was all right to be hurt, so I cried and felt better. They showed me through their own experiences and through my previous relationships that I could make it with or without Lorenzo.

Mr. Parker and some of the girls sat me down and asked me to make a list of my goals. I still have that list:

1. Have a healthy baby
2. Go back home to Lorenzo
3. Get a job

Nowhere in my goals did I mention school or a career. They didn't point it out to me right then. But up until this very day they have been helping me set better goals for myself and my child. With their love and support I've learned to be a stronger black mother and a much better person. My goals are much higher now:

1. Try my best to raise my son right, give him the right values and morals in life.
2. Graduate in January 1994, and go on to a four-year college in the fall of 1994
3. Get my masters degree in child psychology, and start my career as a child psychologist
4. Buy my son and myself our first home
5. And then maybe, just maybe, find a good husband who must also be a good stepfather

I can remember the discussions we would have when we went to talk in the community. We would share stories about what happened when we found out we were pregnant. After we were finished, the audience would ask questions. For younger kids we would play a game called Sexual Jeopardy, which was like Jeopardy, but the questions were about sexual facts and myths. Or we did a skit. For the older kids we would usually have group discussions.

There was a time when I left the program. I had a bad experience with one of the groups I was talking to. They asked questions that were very personal, and they even got nasty when asking them.

I remember one of the young people asking me, "How do you feel now that you have to grow up with your baby?" The kids made me feel stupid and depressed. They had me thinking about living in a shelter and they made me wonder why I was having my son.

The other mothers in the group understood. They told me to take the time I needed to decide if I could continue sharing my experiences as a pregnant teen. After I had my son, I returned to the program.

I decided to return because I had a long talk with Mr. Parker. He helped me realize that I could really help support another pregnant girl who is going through the things I went through and am still going through. The most important thing of all was that I realized that I needed the support of the program for myself.

I am still with the Mentor's Program, and my dependency on Lorenzo has changed. You see, Lorenzo and I broke up a month after my son was born. It hurt and it still hurts (six months later), but at least now I am more self-sufficient than I was before. I am going to school, working with the Mentor's Program, and with my mother's help I am raising my son to the best of my ability.

I know now that when I'm confused and hurt I can get help from someone who cares instead of not facing it. I think we all need support from somewhere. It doesn't matter whether it's a friend, a counselor, or a support group like mine, as long as someone is there to pick us up if we fall.

❏

Anzula B. Richardson, 17, is now living in the South. If there was one thing she had the power to change, it would be "the minds of society, so that children in foster care won't be teased." One of her goals as a writer is to "help prevent people from going through some of the things I went through. My peers seem to learn from me better than from adults."

PEER PRESSURE AND ME

Craig Jaffe

"Yo, Craig, are you down for smoking some buddha tonight?"

"Chill, not tonight, I'm too tired."

"Ah, come on."

"Chill, I said not tonight."

"Fine, b-tch."

"I'll be a b-tch, at least I don't survive on weed alone."

"Shut the f-ck up."

"Yeah, whatever, just get out of my room."

"Yo, don't ever say sh-t to me again!"

"Trust me, I won't!"

Everybody in my group home was going to smoke weed that night. I was the only one who refused, but I didn't say no because I was tired. I refused because I was being pressured into doing something that I was trying to break away from.

Each time the word *no* came from my mouth, I was losing friends. One by one they cursed me out and then left. But if my friends couldn't take no for an answer, then they weren't friends from the get-go.

Peer pressure was trying to take control of my life and I was fighting back. Every time I came face to face with it, I was determined to stand my ground.

Soon I had nobody to turn to in the group home but staff. I would talk to them about the things that I used to talk about with my friends, such as work, girls, sex, drugs, etc. We'd talk about these things and they'd give me advice on how to deal with them.

When my peers noticed I was talking with the staff, they started to call me "teacher's pet," "a--licker," and stuff like that.

Even though I didn't show it, this hurt me deep inside. The staff knew what the other kids were saying and told me to ignore them because they weren't heading anywhere in life except for the men's shelter.

The kids tried to turn everyone in the house against me. They would say things about me to the new kids in the home, and I wanted to fight them.

But I knew that was exactly what they wanted, so there was only one thing I could do—ignore them.

The other kids in the home began to steal things from me. They'd steal anything from personal hygiene stuff to underwear.

One time the whole house ransacked my room. They stole tapes, bottles of cologne, clothes, jewelry, etc. The staff couldn't stop them, but they did help me get my stuff back.

After that incident, all the feelings that I had inside of me finally came to light—hatred, sadness, and anger. But I knew for a fact that I wasn't going to let these feelings take over my life and ruin it. No time soon was I about to give up. I was going to go out like a trooper, not like some damn wimp who couldn't control his feelings.

It took a year for my peers to realize that they couldn't scare me into doing anything I didn't want to do. After they finally learned this, things changed between us. They respected me for who I was, and I respected them for who they were.

Today there are still kids in the house who can't stand me but I don't care, because they aren't paying my bills or putting food in my stomach. So when they tell me they don't like me, I just tell them, "That's a personal problem," and walk away.

Nowadays things are much quieter for me in the group home. Once in a while the kids like to bother me, but it is only out of fun. The tension has eased up. Not everybody in the house is my friend, but I get along with everybody.

The main thing I learned out of this is to have confidence in myself and not to put myself down because of the things other people say or do to me. I don't have to follow other people just to be down, and if people can't respect my wishes and rights, then that's their problem, not mine.

Peer pressure will always exist. Even though I seem to have defeated it, I haven't. It will continue to haunt you and me, and we have to keep fighting it. But by not giving into my peers, I've gained self-esteem and self-respect.

❏

Craig Jaffe, 15, is also the author of "My Crew Was My Family" in the "Family" section of this book.

KICKED TO THE CURB AT TWENTY-ONE

Rick Bullard

I ndependent Living should be run like a military Boot Camp, because only that kind of tough training is going to prepare us for the stress we're going to experience in the Real World. It's the only way to overcome the false sense of security and dependency that the system fosters (no pun intended). We think we're always going to be taken care of, but at twenty-one you are out!

For those who still don't understand, I repeat—at twenty-one, it's over! Your ass is kicked to the curb like an old pair of Lottos! Outta here like last year! Ejected quicker than an M. C. Shan tape! Thrown away like an oregano blunt!

Get it?

When I first moved into my Independent Living facility, I didn't think about that day. I was about to turn eighteen and didn't give a damn about anything, except the money I had in my pocket.

In my first week there, I saw that a lot of the residents didn't have a program and were waiting around to be given one, whereas I, a total maverick, made the effort to find a job within my first week, which I kept for the next year.

For that year I pretty much took care of myself. All I did was club, sleep, and work. Not a care in the world—no drugs, no booze, just a phunkadelic free-flow of peace rhythms and grooves. To work, to club, to sleep, day after day.

The reason I'm telling you this will become apparent as I skip ahead three years to my last year in the facility. By now I was quickly approaching twenty-one and began to realize that the jig was almost up. I should have been saving money, but no one had stressed to me, in a way that would sink in, how important that was. People had told me to save, but not why or how.

So there I was a month before "aging out"—no money, no prospects, no future. Not to mention that I also had nowhere to go after discharge. Ironic, isn't it? I felt like a deer caught in the head-lights of a semi-truck: doomed.

Oh well, I figured I could go play on a freeway and hope for a quick end.

It was then that I remembered what I was when I first came into foster care: a survivor. No matter what it took, I would survive. So I grudgingly moved into my mother's one-bedroom apartment in Brooklyn and it is here that I currently reside with mom and my eleven-year-old sister.

Oh, and by the way—did I mention that I sleep on the couch?

I don't intend on staying here.

That's my plan. That's the whole secret to Independent Living in the first place—have a plan! Hell, have six damn plans! Just in case your main plan falls through, have a set of contingency (that means backup) plans. (Pay attention—you'll be tested on this later, trust me.)

I wished I had more of a plan back when I was in I.L. I wished I had learned to save money. I wished I had gotten some sort of on-the-job training, so that I could support myself with a skill. I would have liked to have had some sort of housing to look forward to, and I wish I had been prepared to go to college.

But none of that happened.

I.L. failed me because it did not consistently and thoroughly train me in the various aspects of living independently.

To be fair, my I.L. facility did have a workshop for people like me who were about to leave in a year. It was actually quite good, because it went into a fair amount of detail on what you needed to do to survive on your own and was led by a facilitator who really knew her stuff (good lookin' out, Carol).

So why did I leave the system unprepared?

Because all this information was crammed into about three months of my final year. The workshop only met once a week for about two hours! I was twenty years old and hearing this stuff for the very first time. I mean, it's almost like you're in the middle of having sex with your partner and he or she suddenly pulls out a condom and say: "Oh honey, we might be needing this." Talk about too little, too late!

To fully prepare me, this workshop should have been given at the beginning of my stay in I.L. and throughout the entire course of my stay there, not as a three-month crash course. In fact, now that I've passed through the system, I know there are many changes that need to be made in how we're prepared to confront the cold, cruel Real World.

One major change should be aimed at those who don't take I.L. seriously. To repeat, Independent Living should be like a god-damned Boot Camp for four years! 'Cause unless you have a trust fund comin' atcha at twenty-one, you better get with the program.

Everyone who comes into I.L. should either be already working or going to school (a fair amount of the residents in my place weren't doing jack). Classes and training should start the moment a participant steps foot in the door of an I.L. facility.

Actually, they should start *waaaaaaay* before that, probably at the age of thirteen or fourteen. An I.L. facility should be the icing on the cake, not a hurried crash course in survival.

From jump, people in I.L. should learn why saving money is so important. When I first got to I.L., they told me to save money. But why should I listen? Give me a reason to listen!

Show me how hard it is to find a fair-priced apartment! Talk to me about security deposits, gas and electric, the cost of hooking up a phone (not to mention budgeting for food, transportation, and clothing)! In my I.L. workshop, everything about housing was too bloody vague.

As far as transitional housing goes, the various apartment programs are fairly useless, unless the residents are actually practicing skills that were taught to them. The people who are accepted into these apartment programs should be already capable of supporting themselves. The apartment programs should be a place for them to *apply* the skills that they learned in I.L., not learn them from jump.

What good is it to house three or four residents in an apartment and pay for their rent, gas and electric, and food? Granted, they'll have to budget their food bill, but the money isn't coming from their own pockets, is it? So in preparing people for reality, that whole situation is rather futile. And at twenty-one they still get the boot.

Those who move into an apartment program should be working and able to carry their own weight as far as rent and the bills go, because they've already been thoroughly prepared by the I.L. facility they came from. When they turn twenty-one, they can move on to true independent living with their own apartment.

We also need specific, tangible job information to help us survive.

I'm talking about practical things, like access to study guides for the civil-service exams. Residents should be encouraged to take federal and state exams so they have at least some prospect for employment.

What can it hurt to have a fee waiver for foster care residents who want to take a civil service test? Look at it this way: those who pass the tests (with study and pre-test help provided by the foster care agencies) will have a chance at becoming employed, and the city, state, and federal governments will have a chance at more taxpayers. It sure as hell beats building yet another homeless shelter.

And since many young people who aren't in foster care now live at home until about twenty-five or twenty-six, I think discharge at twenty-one is bogus—but that's another story.

In closing, the main point I'm trying to impress upon you is that you must develop your own drive to survive, because one day soon the system will bid your behind a cold farewell.

Don't ever let yourself be lulled into a false sense of security. Always remember that just because you are getting money from foster care now, it does not mean you'll be getting it forever. Always have a plan of your own and do what is necessary to help yourself. Let the system help you, but don't let it live for you.

A realistic Independent Living program, combined with your will to succeed, just might enable you to live comfortably. But since I only kick sh-t that I know, I'll leave that "living" topic for another day . . .

❏

When Rick Bullard wrote this article, he was 21 and a seven-year foster care veteran. He says that one of the biggest concerns of foster care youth "isn't about what happens while you're in foster care, but about what's going to happen to you after the cutoff date: the dreaded twenty-first birthday syndrome." Rick has made a successful transition to the "real world": he now has his own apartment, has earned an associate's degree, and works as an assistant librarian at the South Bronx Human Development Organization.

MY GROUP HOME
SCAPEGOAT

Angela Rutman

"*That's why your mother left you in McDonald's with a Happy Meal, you stupid b-tch.*"

"*At least I have a mother.*"

"*Who's your father, Ronald McDonald?*"

These are a few of the insults that are thrown into Jasmine's face almost every day in our group home, but that's not where it ends.

I've been in the same placements with Jasmine (not her real name) for over a year, and I've come to realize that everybody takes their anger out on her.

One girl will get into an argument with Jasmine, then that girl's friends will make it into a bigger argument. Most of the time, Jasmine ends up getting jumped.

One time they trashed Jasmine's room after she got into a fight with them. They ripped down her posters and pulled the head off her stuffed animal. They threw her clothes into a pile and pissed on them, and then they peed on her bed.

From that time on, I felt pity for Jasmine.

I have to admit that I haven't always treated Jasmine much better. Many times I've taken my anger out on her.

I was quick to argue with Jasmine because I knew the rest of the girls would be on my side. It made me feel superior to her. Sometimes I was glad to see her get picked on, as long as it wasn't me they were dissing.

I stopped teasing her after I realized why I was doing it. When I was living back home, I got verbally trashed by my father all the time. He would call me "white trash" and a "fat, lazy b-tch."

I realized that many kids who've been verbally abused or neglected by family members will take out their anger on weaker kids. It's a vicious cycle that needs to be stopped.

But other girls in my group home don't seem to realize why they do it or make up excuses. It's easy for them to pick on Jasmine because everyone is already against her.

Most of the girls say that Jasmine starts it off by getting an attitude with them. I always point out that her attitude is a result of all the abuse she takes.

"Why should she be nice all of a sudden?" I ask the girls. "She knows that in the next five minutes you'll be getting your f-cked-up attitude with her."

She was much weaker and quicker to have a breakdown in our previous placement. She's much stronger now because of all of the stuff she's been through. She's learned how to stick up for herself.

But because she had a weak personality before, people are used to taking advantage of her. Even the new girls talk down to Jasmine because they know they can get away with it.

Most scapegoats have been abused all their lives and don't know how to stop it. A lot of times I actually see Jasmine feeding into it. If people aren't dissing her or arguing with her, then they're not talking to her at all. So she'll do things to start arguments. Maybe scapegoats like the negative attention. Maybe the negative attention is better than no attention at all.

The abuse Jasmine takes won't end soon. Maybe she won't get into any more fights, but she'll still be the one excluded from conversations. Girls will still dis her and make her feel unwanted, but I plan to be on her side.

❏

Angela Rutman, 16, is also the author of "Why I'm Better Off in Foster Care."

A THREE-POINT SHOOTER

Max Morán

You know what's the worst part of living in a group home? I'll tell you. It's getting based on points. In other words, if I'm a good boy I get the right amount of points. But if I'm a naughty kid, I get a big fat "0" on my point sheet. If I get zeros, it means that I will not get more than $2 for allowance, and nowadays $2 is barely enough for two condoms.

Maybe the worst part is the food. I mean it seems like we eat the same thing every other day. Macaroni and cheese and chicken and sometimes I can see the redness in the chicken. I got a strong stomach, but this sight makes me wanna throw up. I just go to my room, blast my favorite CD, take a shower, and go to sleep on an empty stomach.

I know what's the worst part. It's the fact that most of our counselors are not able to fulfill their duties. One counselor who works on weekends, all he does is sleep on the couch all day until it's time for him to go home. Another talks on the phone all night long and another loves arguing. And I love arguing, too. It helps me get rid of all that frustration.

Oh, yeah! Let me tell you about my senior counselor. All she does is sit her behind in her chair and do nothing. Whenever we need something, it always takes her so long to get it for us. She forgets things a lot. I remember one time she forgot to cook dinner. She's a very good person at heart, but she's just not helping us enough.

I do admit that there are one or two counselors who are real cool. There's one who I can talk to about anything, on any level. He can be serious and funny at the same time. I'll call him Jim.

One time I was watching TV and Jim turned the TV off because everybody else didn't do their chores. I just went crazy. I threw the chair I'd been sitting in all the way across the living room and went upstairs to my room and blasted my radio. My senior counselor was right there when this happened, yet she didn't come to speak to me. I can't believe she didn't have five minutes to speak to me. I'm not even worth five minutes? Soon Jim came to my room and started to talk to me. I just told him that all I wanted to do was watch TV. I mean, this summer I'm working basically all day long. If I can't come home to a decent hot meal, at least let me watch TV. Soon Jim apologized and we gave each other a pound and everything was chill.

Maybe the worst part of living in a group home is that we only get $120 for clothing money, and on top of that the check is always two months late. Maybe the most humiliating thing is that we have a pay phone in the kitchen which sometimes doesn't take quarters, so we can only take incoming calls.

There are so many things wrong in this house. When I get time to cook something, I have to go through hell because the stove doesn't always work. Maybe the thing that gets on my nerves the most is that this resident is on the phone with like five different girls. The sad part about it is that he doesn't get any. Any other crazy kid in here would have gotten some from all five of those girls. Sometimes I feel like killing him just for some phone time. I'm a very quiet person, but I guess really bad persons are the quiet type.

Or maybe the worst part of living here is that I'm going through a great depression and yet none of the counselors seems to care. When I'm sad, all I do is sit outside my house on the steps and just cry. I put my hands over my face so people that pass by won't see me crying. Yet I never found any shame in crying.

Other times I go to my backyard with a basketball in my hand and just shoot three-pointers. The longer the distance I shoot from, the better. I always make things hard on myself. That's how my life has been to this day. I'm always trying to shoot three-pointers when I should be making layups. God knows I shoot so many airballs, but someday I'll be a good three-point shooter. Someday.

❑

Max Morán, 18, was born in Honduras and came to the U.S. at age 10. He lived with his family in the Bronx before entering foster care at 15. A resident of a Staten Island group home for several years, Max has now moved into a supervised apartment program in Manhattan.

SHORT TAKES: IF I RAN FOSTER CARE . . .

TRAIN THE COUNSELORS RIGHT

Anita Nieves, *15, New York, N.Y.*

F irst of all, I would change the attitudes of the counselors. I think they should be trained properly, because most of them do not act as if they are. They should at least show some concern and care, even if they dislike the student's ways, because how are you going to keep a child from going AWOL or roaming the streets if you don't give them the attention they need?

I would change the way the facilities look, because a child will act better in a homey environment. For instance, I would put up less posters about the rules and slogans. In the bedrooms I would not have dull and depressing colors, because that also affects the child's performance in the house. I would have bright colors, like blue and orange, etc.

The food! I would make sure the food is of nutritional value and looks appetizing so that the residents would want to eat it.

Then come responsibilities. Residents should be made responsible for their home, room, and the conduct of their peers, so they feel as if they are important to themselves and others.

Next is the issue of criticism. It is *very important* that staff and residents do not criticize each other, because extensive criticism causes them to feel very low about themselves and they will achieve very little. There should be greater encouragement.

Once a month one resident from each facility would go to

speak with the director to say what the residents feel about their situation, whether it be a complaint, request, or compliment. This would help make sure that the residents get some of what they request and that way we can change the reputation and image of the group homes. Maybe the person who directs the CWA will read this and take into consideration what is written here and make the needed changes.

A GYM IN EVERY HOME

Anthony McMahon, *16, Queens, N.Y.*

F irst I would set up about ten big group homes in each borough—five coed, three all-boys, the other two all-girls. The homes would hold up to 150–200 people. I would have twenty-four-hour security. I want counselors who wouldn't just be there for the money but who would have good, friendly relationships with the kids.

The cooks would be professional cooks with a history of good cooking. Every week the menu would change. On holidays I would have all the homes prepare a special feast. I would have job training and after-school classes teaching the kids trades and other different skills to survive out in the world.

I would have people working under me to help the kids find an apartment or a different home to suit their needs. There would be a gym at every home, open 24/7 for the kids to stay occupied. The allowance would be stretched to $30. When the kids first enter the home, they would be given an account. Ten dollars of the thirty would be put into their account every week. They would get this money when they were discharged.

Each child would receive $250 and go shopping with a counselor every six months. If the child wasn't attending school or making an effort to get herself together, he or she would not be awarded these privileges.

I would have a basketball, football, ping-pong, and jump-rope team in every home. I would have a tournament every year for all the different sports listed. This tournament would go on throughout the whole year. This would keep the kids occupied, and a lot of them wouldn't go to jail or go upstate.

YOUR TRUE FRIEND

Brooke Montgomery, *15, Hamburg, N.Y.*

I feel that all people are equal and we all have feelings. When it comes down to foster parents and group home staff, I think that they should understand the young people they take care of. They should always make sure to make time to sit and talk to the kids when they need to talk.

Staff and foster parents should have a good sense of humor to always keep the smiles on their faces. They should always be there to listen to the kids and be able to always do for them. They should also make sure the kids always get a good education and have clothing on their backs and food in their stomachs.

I know how it is in a group home. I live in one now and I see and learn a lot every day. It's hard nowadays to be a kid. You get tricked and fooled by so many people. I think your true friend is yourself.

THE LOVABLE CHILD

Miranda "Nikki" Kent, *15, Harvest, Ala.*

I am fifteen and have been in foster care for three years. I also have a younger brother age four and a younger sister age five who are also in foster care.

As an older child I can pretty much fend for myself, but I feel that the system should be changed to get younger children out of the system and into stable, loving families. There have to be good families out there who would love to have young children to raise as their own.

Parents should not be given children as long as they are still struggling to get their acts together. More consideration should be given to the feelings of the children and the long-term effects on them when they are moved from pillar to post.

Physical cruelty you can get over, but mental abuse lasts forever.

I love my parents and know that they are on drugs and can't seem to help themselves, much less us, but why should my brother, sister, and I have to be punished for their actions? How much of a chance should they be given before we are given a chance?

I have been through a lot in my life and I have been very lucky in finally getting to the foster home that I am in now. They love me for me and treat me just like they do the rest of their kids. They are not in it for the money but because they really care.

But I can't help but think about the kids that are not this lucky. What about the foster care givers who feel that food on the table and a roof over your head are enough? What about feelings, loving, and caring?

What about the children who are too small to speak up when the foster parents are always called first before the agency comes for a pop-in visit? (They always have time to clean up their act or threaten a child to be on their best behavior.)

Does the agency really know what's going on when they call in advance of their visits? Do the people who work at the agency have a family and family experiences? Do they know how children really feel and what the "best interest" of the child is?

You don't learn love from a book but from experiences.

As to how foster parents can be better selected, I think a more in-depth study as to why people want to have foster children should be done. Are their own children well-behaved? Are they treated well? Do they do well in school? Is the family a warm, loving family? Do they really love helping children? Or are they just in it for the money?

If the staff in group homes were hired because they truly love children and not because of the salary, it might not be so bad. If they truly cared for and loved the unlovable child, that child could become lovable. Most children don't act—they react.

I don't think that group homes should be so large, but be more like a true home environment. Maybe like a family that extends to take in other children (like foster families).

I think it would be nice if group homes were set up like the children's home in Decatur, Alabama, a real house with a family and four to six foster children. There are a lot of people who would take foster children if they had the room. They don't have the money to take in children. The State doesn't pay them enough money to cover the expenses of the child, much less additional expenses.

If the State could build houses for these families in regular housing areas, not projects where they would be singled out, and pay a small salary plus room and board, more people would take children. There might even be homeless families who would appreciate a place to live and the opportunity to care for children.

I know that I don't have the answers, but there has to be a better way. I'm only a kid, but maybe by the time I'm grown there will be a better way and other children won't have to go through what my brother, sister, and I have gone through. Maybe all children with parents who don't love them or who can't care for them will have the chance to live as part of a real family with all the love and security of knowing that they are loved, and that no one will come and move them any minute.

Maybe these children will have the opportunity to have real parents to call their own, where they can love and be loved in return. I'm one of the lucky ones.

III
WHO AM I?

TO WHOM IT MAY CONCERN

To whom it may concern.
I'm a sophomore at Curtis
  High.
I don't really like school, maybe
that's why I'm not doing fine.
I wish I was like everybody else.
Sometimes I feel like I'm being
observed by everyone else.
I'm different, and I just want to
write this. To whom it may
concern.

To whom it may concern.
Soon I'll turn sixteen.
Too old to be a baby.
Too young to be a king.
To whom it may concern. I'm
lost in my own world.
I feel like in my young life
I already have failed.
It's lonely, it's sad, it's tough,
when you don't even know
  yourself.

To whom it may concern.
I still believe in God, although
I lose faith in Him sometimes.
To everybody my heart is open.
Maybe that's my problem, that's
why my heart has been so many
times broken.
To whom it may concern.
I'm already losing my family,
I'm also afraid I will lose my
friends.

To whom it may concern.
I want to share the love that in
my heart I have found.
One day I can feel so happy,
the next I can feel like such a
clown.

To whom it may concern.
I have come to realize
that I'm still very young.
I have a lot of things to learn.

I just thought I'd write this to
someone,
or to whom it may concern.

—Max Morán, 18

HOW I LIVED
A DOUBLE LIFE

Omar Sharif

F or most of my life I felt different from the "normal" kids. They had parents and families but I didn't, because I lived in a group home.

We'd have assignments in elementary school and if we didn't finish them in class, the teacher would say, "When you go home tonight, ask your parents to help you."

No one knew how hurt I was by that simple remark. It was not my parents but a counselor who would help me with my homework that night.

I was embarrassed by my situation and I began to hide my identity. I was almost two people in one. During the day in school I pretended I was like everyone else, but at night I could be myself, just a "regular" kid in the group home.

It was uncomfortable to go to Parent-Teachers Night because the counselors who went with me weren't my parents. Now when I look back this seems funny, but at the time it was as serious as life and death.

I'd run into my fellow students on those nights and they would ask, "Hey, is that your mom?" or "Is that your dad?" And I would say something off the topic to avoid the question, like, "Do you think you're gonna get in trouble tonight?" That would always change the subject.

I used to practice gymnastics after school at the YMCA. One afternoon when my session was over, a counselor came to pick me up in the group home van, and as it pulled up, a friend asked me, "Is that your van you're gettin' in?"

I was caught on the spot and didn't know how to respond. So I told him, "Nah, that's a friend of mine who works with a cab service." I hoped he believed me and wouldn't ask me any more questions as I stared him in the face. I guess he thought it was the truth, because he never mentioned it again.

I almost blew my cover one morning when I was picked up at the group home by the school bus. There were twelve of us living there. I was ten years old at the time and also the youngest in the house. The oldest kid was seventeen. I and two other young kids, Wesley and Robert, used to get picked up by the bus at 7:15 every morning to go to elementary school. The rest of the older guys left the house around 7:30 to walk to high school, which was only a couple of blocks away. But this morning my bus didn't show up on time. I went back inside to tell the counselors what had happened, then waited on the steps. At 7:30 the bus came down the block to pick up Wesley, Robert, and me. At the same time, the older guys came out of the group home to walk to school.

I never worried about the kids on the bus seeing me each morning with Wesley and Robert. I always assumed that the kids on the bus thought the group home was my own private house. Wesley could pass for my brother any day because we had the same complexion (we're black), the same haircut, and sometimes we used to dress alike. And Robert, who was Puerto Rican, seemed like a friend hanging out with us.

But now, as the kids on the bus watched, the older high school kids were coming out of the group home and they were white, black, Spanish, and Chinese. It was obvious they weren't my family. As soon as I got on the bus I knew someone was going to question me about the older kids. I could see the puzzlement on their faces as everyone's head was turned to look. So I blurted out an explanation. I told them the older kids were my brothers. Since some of the older guys were black, I hoped the kids on the bus would assume they were my brothers and the rest of the guys were my brothers' friends. But I was so humiliated by the lie that I buried my face in a book in the back seat.

When I was in junior high I usually took the bus, but when I woke up late or overslept I had to be driven to school in the group home van. I remember how ashamed I would be when I was dropped off that way. The kids in my junior high had parents with lots of money. They were all middle class or above. They had good-looking cars, and there I was getting dropped off in a big blue van.

To cover myself, I'd always ask the counselor to drop me off a block away from school. Then I'd wait until the traffic was moving before I got out so none of the students across the street would see me.

I kept where I lived a secret because I was afraid the students would make fun of me. Only one kid knew. How Joseph found out I'll never know. But he was cool—he never told anyone my business, and as a matter of fact, we became close friends because I started to hang out with him. His family was so understanding they even wanted to adopt me. Joseph's mother used to pick me up in her car on weekends to bring me to their house and then drop me back at the group home at night.

Joseph once told me I could stay with his family if I ever needed a place. He was a true friend because he offered me his home when I was down and out. He was someone I could trust, someone I could confide in, someone who knew me and didn't feel ashamed to be around me because I lived in a group home.

Joseph never singled me out—I was a regular kid whenever I was with him. And my main point is that I just wanted to be accepted in the same way by my peers.

As I grew older and became more mature, I began to see that I didn't need to be ashamed about my situation. I began to realize that people looked at me for who I was, not for where I lived or who I lived with. If people liked me before they knew I lived in a group home, they probably wouldn't change their attitude once they found out.

I also realized that "normal" and "regular" kids who live at home are often ashamed of *their* parents. (I don't know why, because all they have in this world are their parents.) You don't have to live in a group home to feel ashamed or awkward, or to feel that you don't really have a family.

My friend Joseph helped me open my eyes and realize that it doesn't matter where you live, just as long as you're true to yourself and to others.

If your friends don't accept you because you live in the system, then they're not your friends and that's their loss. If you are proud of who you are, there will be many more true friends for you down the road of life.

❏

Omar Sharif, 20, is the author of two other pieces in this collection, "My Foster Mother Is My Best Friend" and "Writing Taught Me about Myself."

WHY NO ONE KNOWS I'M A FOSTER CHILD

Shaniqua Sockwell

Do you know how it feels to see other couples walk past you embracing, hugging, and kissing, and not get that same kind of affection for yourself?

Believe me, I do! But I'm not the only one—a lot of teenagers feel the same way. It comes to the point that unless you're "hooked up," you're stuck in a lonely situation for a while.

But this story isn't about my loneliness because I'm not "hooked up." It's about being lonely because I won't give affection to someone I like because that person may find out something about me that will ruin the relationship completely.

This "something" is finding out I'm a foster child. None of my friends know that I am one.

I remember when my foster sister almost blew my cover. I brought a female friend to my home and my foster sister came into the living room and asked me for something. While I was getting it, my friend looked at my foster mother's wedding album and said, "You don't look like your parents at all." My foster sister said, "That's because they're not our . . ."

I didn't have to guess what was coming out of her mouth next. I ran in the living room, covered her mouth, excused us, and gave her a verbal lashing. I told her to never tell anyone that we're foster kids, because then we won't be treated the same way as everyone else. She gave me this are-you-crazy? look, but agreed.

That was the last time I ever brought friends to my house. My foster mother doesn't understand why I don't bring anyone to the house anymore!

Hiding my identity, especially from my friends, is difficult, and unless you've been in my shoes, you don't know how difficult. You don't know how many stories and lies I've told people. I've had to lie about why me and my foster sister look nothing alike, about why I never talk about my family much, and about how I suddenly appeared in my home out of nowhere at the age of ten.

I remember when some of my friends were talking about their families. They asked me about my family and how I liked living in the Bronx (they knew that I had moved to Brooklyn from the Bronx, but they didn't know why). I told them I felt sick and excused myself. They never asked me about my family again. I was afraid they would judge me because of what had happened in my past.

Now, the situation with boys. Hiding my situation from boys is even harder than hiding it from friends. They usually want to know about everything (no offense) and if you get touchy about a certain thing, they'll start going off on you. That's why I make sure I don't get touchy, I just avoid their questions.

Once I was talking to a boy who I thought understood me. I think he knew something was wrong, because when he asked questions like, "Why don't you talk about your family or nuthin?" I would get scared and change the subject. (That's one of the things that makes me feel bad—I *want* people to understand me, but I'm also afraid to get too close.)

He was the first boy I was going to tell I was a foster kid, but I soon came to realize that his concern about my situation was nothing but an act. I caught him talking behind my back one day. I didn't confront him. Instead, I walked away from him and never said anything else to him again.

Then there was Jonathan, who was nosy and went so far as to ask my foster mother why I had suddenly arrived in my family. Jonathan asked my foster mother more questions, and finally one day I told him that if he couldn't mind his own business, he could leave. I lost his friendship because I didn't want to answer questions about my past.

My feelings about holding everything inside haven't changed that much during the six years I've been in care. There are times when I think I'll go crazy if I keep hiding my identity. But if I tell people I'm a foster child, I'm afraid they'll label me and say things like, "She's nobody special."

I'm very lonely and this has its ups and downs. The up is that you don't get your heart broken by someone who doesn't understand what you've been through. The down is that you don't experience first-hand the feeling of caring for someone in a loving way.

Yet a part of me still believes that someone who really cares for me will come along and I won't be afraid to tell that person I'm a foster child. It may take a while, but it will happen.

❏

Shaniqua Sockwell, 16, is also the author of "Questions Without Answers" in the "Family" section of this book. About this story, she says: "Not telling people you're in foster care isn't a bad thing, but you must face the truth sooner or later. It took me a long time to do it, but in the end I became stronger. I can now look at myself and say, 'Yes, I was in foster care, but I'm just like everyone else.' People don't shy away from me, they accept me. And that's all I ever really wanted."

KEEPING IT ON THE DOWN LOW

Lenny Jones

H ave you ever been in one of those situations where you met someone and just knew you would connect? (And not just with certain parts of the body that don't belong in or on another person's body in the first place?) You told that person everything, but when you decided to tell him or her where you lived, your lines got disconnected.

This has happened to a lot of young people in foster care. It even happened to me.

On my first day of high school, I met this girl named Stacie. I wasn't really paying any attention to her 'cause I thought she was shy. A few days later, I saw another side of her and I liked it.

She wasn't nowhere near shy. She was funny, smart, kind, calm, and collected (not saying that shy people are not funny and smart, but they seem to be anti-social). I felt I could tell her anything, but I just couldn't tell her I lived in a group home.

I know it may not sound right, but I was ashamed of my address. I felt I didn't belong there because it wasn't my fault I never had a real family life. I didn't want to be treated differently than anybody else because I was in a group home.

Usually people think that if you're in an all-boy's group home, either you're gay or out for only one thing (sex, if your mental capacity is as fast as a snail). I'm neither.

I wasn't sure what Stacie believed about guys in group homes until one day when we were walking to the train station after a long, agonizing day of school. As we were waiting for the train, she told me she would never go with a guy from the local group home.

As soon as Stacie said that, I felt like my whole life passed before me *(Zzzzz!)*. I stood there motionless and for a second I was in a total blackout. When I came to my senses, I felt soakin' wet (no, I wasn't having a wet dream) from the sweat pouring from my body.

A few minutes later she asked me where I lived and I told her I lived on Beach First Street (not my group home's address, which is a hundred blocks the other way). For a while Stacie believed me.

We even hung around outside my group home and she didn't know I lived there. I told her that I had a lot of friends who lived there. Since I was cool with a lot of the residents, I made sure none of them blew up my spot.

Things were going great until the cook blew up my spot. This is what happened.

That week I was supposed to help cook dinner for the apartment and I forgot. I was buggin' out with Stacie and some of our friends right in front of my group home.

Suddenly, the cook came outside and yelled "Get upstairs!" I tried to play it off like he wasn't talking to me. Stacie and I continued to do positions on a car (for those with nasty minds, we were doing wrestling moves with all our clothes on).

The cook came up to me and said, "Get upstairs, you were supposed to help me today!" I was embarrassed as hell. I just wanted to swing on him but I didn't.

I told Stacie that I'd be right back. The cook butted in and yelled, "No, you're not." So I walked with the cook into the hallway and told him that Stacie didn't know I was in a group home. The cook said it was too late now.

I didn't speak to the cook for weeks. Later that day I asked my friend what Stacie said when I left and he told me that she called me "a little group-home boy." After he told me that, all my hopes and dreams of having a relationship with her were gone with the wind.

The next day, Stacie told me she had a feeling I was in a group home. It was quite obvious. Stacie wondered why I was coming to school from the wrong direction, when I told her I lived about twenty blocks away in the opposite direction.

Stacie and I had a little talk about my living situation and her comment, which hurt me a lot. We resolved it, but after that incident I tried not to let anybody know I was in a group home.

But I got caught out there another time with this girl named Ja-Keya. She didn't know I was in a group home.

She gave me her number and I called it about three times but no one was home. Later that day staff told me my girlfriend called. So I'm wondering to myself, *It can't be Ja-Keya 'cause she doesn't have my number.* I thought staff were trying to play me.

I called Ja-Keya and I asked her how she got my phone number and she said, "I got Caller I.D."

The first thing that came to mind was, *Oh, damn, she knows where I live. Time to get dumped again.* I felt this way because whenever someone calls the group home, it has to go through the switchboard. The first thing the operator says is, "Hello, So-and-so Home for Boys, may I help you?"

While we were on the phone, I was just waiting for Ja-Keya to say those two little words every man hates to hear—not "I'm pregnant" but "It's over." (I thought she'd be another Stacie.)

What surprised me was that Ja-Keya didn't say that. Instead, Ja-Keya made me realize that not all relationships are based on where you live. Instead, they're based on who you are.

Unfortunately Ja-Keya didn't really care about me ("must be the money"). So we decided to go our separate ways. Our relationship ended, but not because I'm in foster care. Ja-Keya treated me like anyone else.

But even to this day, not too many people know about my double life. I choose to keep my whereabouts on the D.L. 'cause being unnecessarily discriminated against and stigmatized (ooh, big words!) more than I am already isn't much fun.

I feel my address shouldn't matter. As long as I have respect for myself and females, I'm just like everyone else (broke!). So what if I've had a few mishaps in my life—I'm trying to go "from negative to positive and it's all good."

❏

Lenny Jones, 16, was born in Brooklyn and entered foster care in 1994. He has lived in group homes in Queens and Manhattan. Lenny plans to become a computer programmer and own his own computer business. He also wants to be a freelance writer in his spare time. His essay, "What They Say Behind Our Backs," follows.

WHAT THEY SAY
BEHIND OUR BACKS

Lenny Jones

W hen I wrote the story "Keeping It on the Down Low," I talked about keeping my whereabouts on the down low in relationships. (I don't want to tell females I like that I live in a group home.)

While writing the article, I became curious if people really have stereotypes about foster care kidz or if that's just a phobia of mine. So I decided to interview six of my classmates in school without telling them I'm in the system.

I asked them what stereotypes they've heard about foster care kidz.

"They run away a lot," said Lynn, 17, "because they don't like the people who they're living with and they're a lot of troubled kids. That's understandable, though."

("Troubled kidz?" Take that back . . . I'm not a kid!)

"They're all messed up and everything. . . . I think that I would be messed up, too, getting ripped from family to family," said Paulette, 16.

(We're people, not chain letters. Better recognize, fool.)

"That they grow up to be troubled, like . . . criminals," said Jose, 16.

(Imagine that!)

"Well, I heard that foster care kids are troublemakers and they're not good people to hang around with," said Hank, 17.

(You hang around with me, and I'm a perfect angel.)

"That they're usually troublemakers, that's what people usually say," said Fawn, 18.

(Isn't that what the last guy said?)

Then I asked them how they personally felt about kidz in foster care.

"I don't think they deserve that, I don't think anybody does," said Lynn.

(I said foster care, not the electric chair.)

"I think it's good, 'cause kids who don't have families can have one and hopefully it will be forever," said Paulette.

(Most of us already have families.)

"I feel sorry for them because they must of not had no good childhood if they're in foster care," said Jose.

(Before you feel sorry for someone, learn some proper English, please!)

"I feel sorry for kids in foster care, but I think it's good . . . they get to have parents," said Vincent.

(So where did we come from if we didn't have parents?)

"They're just regular kids," said Hank.

(Amen.)

"I have nothing against them, but some of them can be troublemakers, some of them can't, depends on the situation they were in," replied Fawn.

(True, true.)

Then I asked them if they would treat someone in foster care differently from other people.

"I don't think they deserve to be treated any different. They're human, they have two eyes, two legs, two feet, one nose, one mouth," said Lynn.

(We get the point, geeeeez!)

"They're like everybody else and they have to be treated the same," said Paulette.

(Right on!)

"No, not if I knew them for a while, if I knew them before they went in there," said Jose.

(No comment.)

"I probably would [treat them differently]. I don't know, because I would feel sorry for them," said Vincent.

(I'm about thissssss tired of people feeling sorry for us. I don't need your sympathy!)

"I would try not to, but subconsciously I would," said Hank.

(This guy doesn't even know what the word means.)

"I wouldn't, but, like [Hank] said, you would do it on accident, you wouldn't mean to do it," said Fawn.

(Accidentally on purpose.)

I also wondered (damn, I'm nosy) if they would ever date someone in foster care.

"Yeah, sure, they're the same as anyone else. Besides, they don't have two steady parents," said Lynn.

(So hold up. Why are you asking about my parents? Are you going out with me or them?)

"Yeah, because they're like any other girl," said Jose.

(Yeah, they're smart enough not to date a guy like you.)

"I don't know, I wouldn't know why not," said Hank.

(I'll get back to ya later.)

"Yeah, I have, because they're people like us, they're ordinary people," said Fawn.

(We're not ordinary, we're extraordinary!)

Last but not least, I wanted to know if they would try to hide it if they were in foster care.

"I wouldn't hide it. I don't think it's anything to be ashamed of," said Lynn.

(That's what she thinks, let her come see my group home for a weekend!)

"I think I'd be ashamed to tell people around school," said Paulette.

(Ya damn right.)

"But if it was like my family or friends, I'd tell them," she added.

(What, that you're still in love with Barney the Dinosaur?)

"I think I'd try to hide it because I'd feel embarrassed not having a parent," said Vincent.

(We have parents, damn it! It's just that they're temporarily out of order. And what's so spectacular about living with biological family, anyway?)

"I guess so, but it's not their fault they don't have parents, so I guess I'd be embarrassed like Victor said," said Hank.

(Why do I have a feeling that he believes that babies are brought from heaven by storks and that Elvis is still alive?)

"It depends on who I hung around with and who I knew. I would probably tell them straight out that I was a part of it," said Fawn.

(You go girl!)

As you can see by their quotes, about half of them don't know what the hell they're talking about. One minute they're saying we're "regular" people, then the next minute they're saying we grow up to be crooks and robbers. (If that's regular, I guess I'm unique).

And I wonder if the people I interviewed who said they would tell others that they're in the system would really do that—nah! It's not that I don't believe them, but it's just that they haven't been in my shoes (about an eight and a half).

They just don't know how it feels. They never had to put up with some residents who are full-time kleptomaniacs and liars. They never had to eat group home food that has no aroma (or taste). And they've never had to try to be independent with little or no help from anybody, even friends.

On the other hand, maybe they wouldn't be embarrassed about being in foster care. Maybe they would like the lack of privacy, all the attention from perfect strangers, the loneliness of not feeling love from family. And, worst of all—the food.

(Before some idiot or Republican—same thing—gets pissed, I'm being sarcastic. Not everything in the group home is bad. The best part is the freedom.)

But after interviewing these six people, I decided that I don't give a damn what anyone has to say about me being in foster care because I expected their replies to be much more harsh (instead of idiotic). Hey, I'm in the system and there's not a damn thing anyone can do about it. I'm not saying that I'm going to broadcast it over the radio, but I'm not going to lie about it either.

KICKED OUT
BECAUSE I WAS GAY

Shameek Williamson

D uring my first four years in foster care, I was in nine group and foster homes. My ninth home was different from the others because I had just "come out" as a gay person and I was worried about being accepted by my new foster mother, Sharon.

When I first moved in with Sharon and her two biological daughters, I kept to myself. I felt close to Sharon but not close enough to tell her I was gay. Since I had just come out, I wasn't sure if this was who I really was or if it was only a stage I was going through. I didn't want to tell Sharon until I was sure I was gay.

Before I moved in with Sharon, I came out to my social worker. She thought Sharon would be an excellent foster parent because Sharon had once been in the system, was young, and could probably accept my sexual identity.

After I moved in with Sharon, I used to go gay clubs by myself or with my friend Carla (who was also gay). I wasn't in a relationship yet and this was my way of exploring the gay scene.

One night at the Octagon, a gay club in Manhattan, Carla introduced me to her ex-girlfriend Bridgette. We only said hello, but I thought about Bridgette throughout the rest of that night and continuously through the week.

The next week I went to Pandora's Box, another gay club, by myself and saw Bridgette. We danced, drank, and at the end of the night exchanged numbers. But because I had just come out, I felt uneasy about having a relationship with another woman.

After about two weeks of talking on the phone, we decided to go out. We first went to a restaurant and, during the next couple of months, Bridgette took me to get my hair done and brought me flowers, basically treating me like no man ever had. By now I knew that being gay was who I really was.

Sharon, who had been worried because I didn't have any friends, became so happy I now had Bridgette that she encouraged us to see more of each other.

But even though I was sure I was gay, I still had to hide it from my foster mother. Even though Sharon had mentioned to me that she had gay friends, I wasn't sure if she would accept me because I was living in her home.

(Some people think it's okay to have friends who are gay because all friends do basically is hang out together, but having them live in their house is different because many people believe that gay people are sex-crazed and jump on everyone who passes by.)

One time Bridgette and I went out and she brought me flowers. When I got home, Sharon saw the flowers and said to me, "You told me that you were going out with Bridgette, but you two went out with guys and he brought you flowers." Nervously, I just agreed with her, wondering how long this charade would last.

Somehow or other Sharon eventually found out that Bridgette was gay and assumed that I was gay also. To this day I really don't know how she found out. (Maybe it was the way I whispered on the phone every time Bridgette called, or the way I went into the bathroom to continue our conversations.)

After Sharon found out, she told my social worker that she didn't want me in her house anymore because she was afraid I would try something with her twelve-year-old biological daughter. When the social worker told me this, I immediately became angry because I would never invade her daughter's privacy in that way.

The moving didn't bother me because I had moved nine times before that and I had learned not to get close to anyone. So I ended up staying with my uncle for a few weeks until my worker found me a new placement. I didn't want to stay in Sharon's house if she didn't trust me.

In the meantime, I noticed Bridgette had slowly started drifting away. I asked her why our relationship was ending. She explained to me that she became frightened because she had destroyed a relationship between a mother and daughter.

(Little did Bridgette know that Sharon wasn't my mother. As with every placement I had, I was ashamed of being in foster care, so I had told Bridgette that Sharon was my real mother. Now I couldn't tell her that Sharon was my foster mother because Bridgette would think I didn't trust her enough to tell her the truth from the start.)

It's been one and a half years since I left Sharon. Bridgette and I still speak every once in a while, but the relationship is over. Sometimes I choose not to admit it, but I do think I loved Bridgette. I have a hard time admitting it because I try to keep my emotions hidden within myself.

But since that incident, I have been honest at the beginning of my relationships. I tell them I'm in foster care, and if the relationship progresses, I tell them things that happened in my past.

I am presently in kinship care with my grandmother. She doesn't know I'm gay because she wouldn't accept it due to her religious beliefs. I can't afford to have her kick me out of the house because I'm nineteen years old and there is no place for me to go. But when I do move out in January I might decide to tell her, because I'll no longer be living under her roof.

As far as Sharon goes, she was wrong for making me leave because of my sexual preference. I would never have tried anything with her daughter. I would never take advantage of anyone like that. Being gay doesn't mean you want to have sex with everyone you pass by.

I think agencies should warn prospective foster parents who are willing to take teenagers that they might have a gay teen in their home, and should give them training on how to deal with those types of situations. Foster care is supposed to accept all youth, no matter what their sexual identity is.

Sharon may have had gay friends, but she couldn't accept a gay person into her family. Sharon may have lived in foster care, but obviously she didn't understand or care how her rejection would affect me. How could Sharon judge me like that if she had once been in foster care herself?

Personally, I'd rather be moved than live a lie, but no one should have to live a lie for fear of being moved.

❑

Shameek Williamson wrote this story when she was 18. She would like to see better training and evaluation for foster parents. "I've noticed that the foster parents I've lived with ei-

ther do it for the money, or they try to replace your natural parents." The first person in her family to go to college, Shameek is studying social work at Audrey Cohen College in Manhattan.

MY FRIEND MARISOL

Angi Baptiste

I remember when I was moved to my second group home in Coney Island. I was so scared that I didn't want my caseworker to leave me and I held onto her very tight. When you're new in a group home, the girls can scare you by the way they look at you when you walk in the front door.

After I met everybody, things were okay. I got along with the girls and the staff. In fact, I became the staff's pet. That's the name some girls called me because all the staff trusted me. I was given special privileges and I was never on restriction.

One day a new resident came to the group home. He walked in the front door with his social worker. He was wearing baggy pants and a shirt and had a hat on. I looked at him with a big Kool-Aid smile on my face. But all he gave me was an up-and-down look.

I rushed downstairs to the basement and told the girls there was a cute guy in the living room. So everybody started going upstairs one by one to check him out. The staff called me and I went upstairs to introduce myself. That's when I was shocked to find out that "he" happened to be a she. Her name was Marisol.

I helped Marisol with her suitcase and showed her to her room. I helped her put away her clothes. The girls were shocked that "he" was a she. They said that Marisol must be a lesbian, and they started talking about how they hated lesbians and gays.

When Marisol came downstairs to watch TV with us, the girls started making fun of her and teasing her. They started asking her personal questions, like, "How do lesbians have sex?" Then they turned off the light and touched her. Marisol got upset and I got upset too.

The thing I was happy about was that Marisol knew how to defend herself. She went upstairs and told the staff how the girls were bothering her.

After she went upstairs the girls were still laughing, and as for me, I was getting angrier and angrier. I was so upset I banged on the table to get their attention. They all got quiet and listened to what I had to say. I told them how wrong it was to make fun of someone just because they are gay or lesbian.

I also told them to think how they would feel if they were lesbian and someone was making fun of them. The residents apologized to Marisol. After that she got along with them.

I was always there for Marisol every step of the way. So was my friend Marjorie. The three of us were like the Three Musketeers. After a while, Marjorie and I both had a crush on Marisol.

Sometimes we would go into each other's room and talk. Marisol would stare at me non-stop and I would do the same.

The staff got on Marisol's case for no reason. They would have arguments almost every night because sometimes she'd get caught flirting with the other girls, or the staff would make fun of her and she would get very upset.

When I stuck up for Marisol, the staff put me on restriction. They would scream at me and tell me to mind my own business. I just ignored them. They would send me to my room and I'd start crying, because it hurt me to see them making fun of Marisol just because she was different.

Marisol would sneak upstairs to my room and talk to me. That always made me feel better. Our relationship was getting closer. We held hands sometimes and when we did, the other girls would tell the staff. The staff would then talk to me and tell me that I was "too pretty and nice" to turn into a lesbian. But I just ignored what they said.

When it came to the point where I was gonna kiss Marisol, that's when the staff destroyed our relationship forever. They said dirty things about me to Marisol. After that, we were no longer as close as we used to be. We started arguing over stupid things.

But I never stopped loving Marisol. I was still there for her and gave her everything. I would buy her teddy bears and give her money every time she needed it.

One time Marisol, the other girls, and I were playing Truth or Dare, and Marisol brought up something stupid. (It's personal.) She wanted me to say if it was the truth, but I didn't want to. So she argued with me and we wound up fighting.

We were choking each other when Marisol looked at me and realized that she was hurting me more than I was hurting her. She walked away and punched the wall because she was angry. As for me, I ran upstairs to my room and cried.

When Marisol came in my room I was doing my homework with tears coming out of my eyes. She saw me crying and she apologized. I did also and she kissed me. That's when I felt better.

The worst part was that Marisol and I never went out. She went out with other girls, but not with me. And those girls never did anything for her. Sometimes I'd catch her kissing other girls and I would get jealous and cry.

I wanted to go out with Marisol because I loved her. I loved her more than anything in the world. I tried many times to explain to her how I felt. She just ignored me, but I didn't give up. I wrote her millions of letters.

I was very surprised to have these feelings for another girl. I never expected to fall in love with Marisol—it just happened. I had never felt that way before about a girl, but I just went with what I was feeling. And I don't think those feelings will ever change because I still have it in me to love another woman.

When Marisol finally realized how much I loved her and cared about her, she told me she could only picture us being close friends because if she went out with me, the staff would put both of us on restriction.

When Marisol left the group home I cried until there were no more tears left. It wasn't even time for her to leave. She just packed her clothes and left cause she couldn't take it anymore with the staff.

Before Marisol left, she gave me her picture and a necklace that she loved very much. Some of the girls cried because she cheered up everybody with fun and laughter.

She picked me up in the air and I felt like I was in heaven. She kissed me, took her stuff, and was gone. All I could do was just stand there with tears falling down my cheeks. Then she came back and gave me another hug and kiss and said goodbye.

About a year after she left I saw Marisol again. We went out to Coney Island and had fun. At that time I was already out of the group home and in a foster home. We visited the group home that we were once in. That was the very last time I saw her.

But I will always remember Marisol. I still love her very much. I never fell in love with a girl before.

When someone is gay, lesbian, or bisexual, that doesn't mean you have to go against them. So what if a girl likes another girl or a guy likes another guy? That doesn't make them any different. They deserve respect like everybody else.

And it doesn't mean you have to stop being their friend or make fun of them, because if it was you, you wouldn't like it.

The only thing that will always be in my heart is how much fun we had together. I'm never gonna forget Marisol's beautiful smile and the way she used to make me laugh. I carry her picture with me all the time. I won't forget her and how much she meant to me.

❑

Angi Baptiste, 17, has lived in a series of foster homes and group homes since 1993. About this story, she says, "I wanted to express my feelings to others and to let them know that feeling the way I did for Marisol is natural. It doesn't make you a bad person if you like someone of the same sex. I wanted to remember Marisol not only in my thoughts but also in my writing."

IS STEALING MY ADDICTION?

Anonymous

A lot of the girls in my group home steal. One day I went with three of them to shoplift. It was the first time that I ever actually planned to go out and steal.

We told staff that we were going to the park, but instead we went to the shopping center around our way.

We took stupid stuff, like nail polish and makeup. I don't even like to wear makeup, but I was racking up the most because I really didn't care if I got caught. Getting caught didn't even seem real to me. I was on a roll.

As soon as we walked towards the door to leave, this big woman security guard came over and said calmly, "Come with me," as if everything was gonna be all right. There was no sense in running because she would have caught at least one of us.

The lady and a man took us into a little room with tons of TV cameras. It was so embarrassing to know that all that time they were watching us.

I couldn't really absorb in my mind that we really had gotten caught. They did a lot of paperwork on us, even down to our height and weight. Then the man called our staff to pick us up.

I'll never forget the look on my staff's face as she walked into the room. Especially when she heard that it was my idea. She never expected me to do such a thing.

What's weird was that I wanted to take credit for being the leader of it all. It gave me the satisfaction of being involved, but not being a follower. Letting my staff know that I was the leader made my crime seem less severe at the time. It made it easier to deal with the punishment.

We lucked out by getting total restriction for only a month. It could have been much worse. My real punishment was having to face everyone who was disappointed in me.

My best friend made me feel like a low life for stealing. Even now she throws what I did in my face when we get into arguments. I can't blame her because she's right. Stealing is wrong, but I can't help doing it.

The first thing I ever stole was candy when I was around seven years old. I stole it from this old man's candy store, a block away from my building.

I can't remember what kind of candy I stole, but I remember having enough money to buy it. I felt guilty so I never stole from him again, but that didn't stop me completely from stealing.

My mother was a thief, so from an early age I learned that stealing was a way of getting over. She stole anything that she could get away with. My mom stole because she felt she had to. It was the only way she knew how to survive.

I learned it and copied it from her, but I stopped stealing once I went into a foster family at the age of eight. I was scared of what my foster mother would do if she found out.

Now I live in a group home. Only a few months ago I started stealing again. I wanted some expensive perfume that I couldn't afford. Since then I've stolen the stupidest things.

Everyone who knows me would be shocked to hear this. Maybe that's one reason I do it. All of my staff and the rest of the girls in the house make me out to be perfect. Maybe the reason I steal is to show them that I'm not perfect.

Sometimes I feel like taking drugs to make me feel better, but I'm scared to do that because drug addiction runs in my family. So instead I steal.

Stealing gives me a natural high. Every time I slip something into my pocket or under my shirt, it gives me the biggest rush. I feel reckless.

I've never stolen from anyone I know because that kind of stealing seems low to me and I would never want to break their trust. Also, I'd rather steal from big department stores. There seems to be a much easier chance of getting caught, and that makes stealing even more fun. It's not that I actually want to get caught, I just enjoy the risk of getting caught.

I think I steal because I have a lot of resentment toward my parents for not allowing me to be a kid. I had to watch them make all the mistakes. I was expected to learn from their mistakes.

I have the type of parents who will light up a joint right in front of my face, but they'll tell me not to try drugs. My mother and father always screwed up, yet they expected me to be perfect. So when I steal, it's like I'm rebelling against my parents.

I don't know if I'll ever be able to stop stealing completely. The problem with me is that even though I know it's wrong, I do it anyway. The fact that stealing is wrong completely vanishes from my mind as I'm about to do it.

I have to admit that I don't even feel guilty about it. Maybe a little embarrassed, though. Why should I feel guilty if the store I'm stealing from loses a little money?

But when something gets stolen from me in my group home, I get really offended.

Once a girl who was leaving for another group home stole my towel. It was just a plain burgundy towel that was given to all of us. If I had caught her, I would have asked her, "What the hell were you thinking?"

I must not make sense to you. I'm telling you one thing but doing another.

Stealing is wrong, no matter how you do it. I consider my stealing a problem. I've been talking to my therapist about why I do it.

As I said before, addiction runs in my family. Drugs aren't the only kind of addiction, and I've realized this because of my father's multiple addictions (gambling, smoking, sex, etc.).

I don't consider my stealing to be a very severe case, but perhaps it stems from a need for self-destruction. In all addictions you are hurting yourself in some way. Because of my past and my family situation, it's as if I need an addiction. It's as if I need to punish myself, but I really don't know why I have that need.

I haven't stolen in a while, and right now I don't want to do it anymore. I'd like to believe that my crime days are over, but who knows what I'll be feeling in a week or even a day from now.

❏

Anonymous, 16, wrote this story in the summer of 1994. "Even though I wrote it anonymously," she says, "it made me feel better. It took a lot of guilt off me by showing people I know I had done wrong. And I haven't had the urge to steal in a long time."

PHAT FLOWS, HONEYS, AND THE BOOMS

Shawan Raheem Samuels

My social worker always claimed she could understand what I was going through. She figured because she was black, she could automatically relate to me. I'd try to explain the fights I was having in the projects. She'd say they were "silly misunderstandings" and that I should try to "reason" with my foes.

So then I asked her: "What if they don't want to reason? What if they still want to fight me?" She said I should walk away and ignore them.

One time I did walk away from a foe because I thought the dispute was settled. As soon as I turned my back, the person I was "reasoning with" hit me from behind with a sucker punch. We all know you can't walk away from a fight in the ghetto. If I do, my friends will label me a sellout and then they'll try to test me.

"Then you should inform the police if someone tries to bother you," my social worker said.

"*What?* Don't you know the rule of the ghetto? My father told me never to snitch, 'cause I could get a stitch."

"You should go to the cops if you have trouble," she repeated.

"That will only make things worse," I replied. "I'll lose my friends, my respect, and I will still have to fight anyway. Nothing will be solved."

We came from two different worlds and she couldn't understand what I was going through. Compare the advice she gave me to the advice I would have given myself. Who would you listen to?

My Social Worker's Advice on Fights and Conflicts:

"You shouldn't hang out on the corner. The guys there are bad influences. When they have fights you should go home and stay home. When guys from other neighborhoods come through your way to start fights, you should walk away. If they want to fight, try to reason. If they don't want to reason, just ignore them and walk away. If they try to harm you, notify the authorities. If your so-called friends believe you are a punk, then let them believe that. Your friends only influence you into causing calamity."

My Advice:

"Well, there is no way you can stay inside your crib and lounge your whole life. You have to pass through the hood someday. You should start ballin' more and stop brawlin'. Take time out from the corner and get some exercise, so you won't be on the lazy tip. I know you got skills on the ball tip, you know what I'm sayin'? Spend more time on those phat flows you be flippin'. Spend more time with the honeys, instead of hanging with the roughnecks.

"When brothers want to step to you, I understand you can't walk away and front. Your peeps would think you're a sellout. If the guy you got beef with can't do you nothin', then dead the beef. Just back off, but don't turn your back, 'cause you will probably get snuffed from behind.

"It's better to just parlay because you can't tell who's packing steel these days. You don't be strapped because you ain't with that no more—you're smart. If they still wanna flip even though you're trying to chill, I guess you're gonna have to do what you gotta do to defend yourself."

My Social Worker's Advice on Relationships:

"Just make sure you use condoms if you are performing sexual intercourse."

My Advice:

"I know how it is with the honeys. You meet them, get the digits, and so on. Or maybe you are swinging a little somethin' with a honey from around the way. You probably flirt with different honeys. I know when you get a honey in the crib, and she's with whatever you feel like doing, you can't front. Sometimes you have to control yourself, my man. Think, if you and a honey swing somethin' in your crib, she just might want to swing a little somethin' on the relationship tip.

"Maybe you might feel you ain't ready for that. You have to think with your mind sometimes. Think about how honey's gonna feel about you, and how you're gonna feel about her. What if she wants to get with you and you dead her? You know that's gonna cause beef. She'll say you used her, and try to slay you. She'll start to gossip about you or try to get another guy to flip a script for her. You gots to parlay, because using girls could cause massive beef."

My Social Worker's Advice on Peer Pressure:

"You shouldn't hang out with your friends anymore. They are no good. How about picking a new crowd to hang out with? These girls that you hang around are no good also. Why don't you start associating with nice college girls who are planning on finishing school? You should stay in your house, study, and avoid your peers. You are a follower, try being a leader for once. Your so-called friends only cause you to do stupid and disrespectful things."

My Advice:

"I know how it is when you grow up with these guys. They've been your peeps for most of your life. Whenever you did something, you did it with your peeps. So you think that whenever they did something, you had to do it too. So when they pressured you into smoking a blunt, you didn't feel like you were being pressured. Little did you know you were being pressured.

"Whatever you went through, your peeps probably went through the same damn thing. You can relate to them; therefore you hang with them. I know you want to get your props in the hood, and you don't want to be left out, you know what I'm sayin'?

"Then you got all these problems stressin' you. You want to

forget about all these problems, so I know you grab a Phillie and a bag of booms and you get open. I know you grab a forty or a Hiney to go with that blunt. You get nice, then you forget about all your problems—until you get sober again. And after that first blunt, you start to get open on the regular.

"You start learning about the different types of booms, such as Chocolate Thai, Skunk, Buddha, etc. The next thing you know, you start spending mad dead presidents on the booms. You gots to lounge on the booms tip. You're always riffin' about being poor, then you go out and spend mad dough on those blunts. I know it's hard to stop once you start. But you could stop—it's all in your mind.

"I know you want to cut school to hang with the fellas and the honeys. You go to these hooky parties and chill. But what happens when you get left back? Your friends ain't gonna make that grade up for you. Then you're gonna disappoint your family. I know you would pick the honeys over school, but I'm sure you would change your mind if you could see into your future. So just do the right thing and don't be a dunce, 'cause you only live once. You know what I'm sayin'?"

❏

Shawan Raheem Samuels, 18, is also the author of "Six Months on the Run from the BCW."

I'M THE MOMMY NOW

Jessica DeSince

I am fifteen and I have a sixteen-month-old son named Edwin who just learned to walk. I love him so much, but being a mother in foster care isn't easy.

I've found it very hard mentally, physically, financially, and emotionally. It gets depressing. Sometimes I feel as though there's no one there for me. But I am a strong black woman and I won't let those things get to me.

I really didn't want to have a baby. It happened because we didn't use any contraceptives. So it's not like I didn't know what I was getting into.

I chose to rough it out without the father, not because I wanted to but because he couldn't be adult about it. He chickened out and told his mother that the baby wasn't his. He bailed out on the both of us.

After my son was born and was about eleven months old, I started hanging out all night long. I was coming home at all hours of the night.

I was living with my grandmother and decided that I didn't want to live by her rules, so I moved into a friend's house. That's why my grandmother put the PINS warrant (Person in Need of Supervision) out on me.

I went into foster care that same night. Now I *had* to live by someone else's rules—or else. So far I've been getting along just fine. All I've got to do is listen.

I've since learned from my foster mother that hanging out isn't all that. My son is more important than staying out late, and my boyfriend comes after the baby. My boyfriend understands because I love him and he knows I do.

Having a baby is no joke. Having a baby isn't like having a doll or holding someone else's baby. When Edwin cries there's no mommy to give him to, because I'm the mommy now.

It's hard! Sometimes there's no one there to give me support. I had to convince myself to stay on top. If you don't, people will pull you down. You have to be patient. You have to be willing to put your child first.

I had my son in July and then September came. Off to school I went and off to the babysitter my two-and-a-half-month-old Edwin went. If I didn't have a babysitter to watch Edwin, I wouldn't be where I am now.

At first it was hard getting up at 5:30 in the morning. But soon it became routine. Wake up, wash up, fix the bottles, fix the diaper bag, wake him up, play put-on-the-shirt-and-the-pants game, wipe him off (I couldn't bathe him because it was too cold), dress him, get my things together, bring him to the sitter, and go to school.

After five grueling hours in school, come home, pick up the baby, feed him, do homework, play with him, feed him again, watch a little TV, then go to bed. And . . . wake up next morning to do it all over again.

You have to be willing to wake up at all hours of the night to comfort the child. Some children are born with a problem called colic. It makes them irritable and cranky. It has to do with too much gas in the baby's stomach. You lose a lot of sleep. I also lost a lot of sleep because I breast fed my son and he woke up every two hours to be fed.

I had to get used to the baby being at home with me and then when I started getting used to it—bam!—it was time to go to school. It wasn't easy, but I did it.

I began to regret my son at one point. I remember it like it was yesterday. It was December of 1993, when it was snowing so hard you couldn't even see your hand in front of your face. It was a Sunday. I was home doing something and Edwin was crying and crying.

I didn't know what was wrong with him. I was going out of my mind with grief. He had diarrhea and he was vomiting, so I decided that I was going to school the next day and if he was the same when I got home, I'd bring him to the emergency room. When I got home the babysitter told me that he was still sick, so I brought him to the E.R. and I found out he was dehydrated.

That means Edwin wasn't getting enough water into his system. You can't give a baby only formula. They need water, too. It doesn't have to be much, just an ounce after you feed them.

When I saw Edwin in the hospital bed with the tubes sticking out of him, I started to cry. The doctors were reassuring me that he would be all right.

Seeing him like that made me think about it. It kinda smacks ya in the head. *"Wake up! Your son almost died!"* I might never have seen my son again. So I praise the Lord that I have him, and I'm sorry for ever regretting him. I never loved my son more than I do today.

Since I haven't been with my baby's father, meeting guys has been interesting. Many guys don't want to get involved with a girl who has a child, because they don't want to get stuck buying diapers.

Either they want to be with you because they think you're "experienced" because you have a baby, or they don't want the responsibility of being a father and having to set an example for the child.

The way I feel about it is, my son is sixteen months old and hasn't had a daddy to buy diapers, milk, toys, and clothes. So I don't need a replacement daddy because I'm the one who will continue to buy the diapers, milk, toys, and clothes.

I love my son. It's hard, yes, but we are going to make it. I'm going to try hard to train him to respect women. And if he ever decides that he wants to be a father, he will be a better one than his father will ever be.

Honestly, even though I had a few minutes of pleasure for five hours of *pain* (no medicine or painkillers), I would do it all over again. But I would change the circumstances so my baby's father would be there for us.

His father now says he believes that Edwin is his son, but that doesn't change things. If he really thought Edwin was his son, he'd be doing things for him.

Instead, Edwin's father doesn't do jack sh-t. When Edwin was born, his father's mother gave the baby a suit and on Christmas he gave Edwin a sleeper. Big deal! A baby can't live off that!

I'm with a terrific guy now who treats me nice and loves me very much. I'm not exactly happier, because all relationships have their ups and downs, but I'm very content. I can see a future for us.

What I have to say to young girls out there is, number one, stay away from these nasty men. Eight times out of ten they only want one thing. Number two, if you don't practice abstinence, use protection. It's not only to protect you from pregnancy, but also from STDs, HIV, and AIDS.

The last thing I have to say is, if you're pregnant, don't let the baby stop you. Look at me—I'm a sophomore in high school and I have a child. I want to be a nurse or a lawyer. As Tupac says, I'm going to keep my head up.

Still, too many people are ignorant about what it takes to be a mother. A girl I know, no more than sixteen, once told me, "I want to have a baby." I said it's not easy and I started to give her a little speech.

She paid me no mind and said she wanted to find out for herself. I looked at Edwin and thought about what we've been through. I looked back at her. I wanted to laugh in her face.

❏

Jessica DeSince, 15, was born in Brooklyn and has lived in a series of foster homes and mother-child placements.

WHO'S THE REAL "PROBLEM CHILD"?

Marcus J. Howell

P roblem children, "hoodlums," the people who end up in either jails or mental homes—these are some of the labels that are tagged on us from the day we enter care.

I am not a label. I am a person who has been labeled all my life and I've always fought it. I hate hearing, "Oh, he's just a foster kid, he doesn't know what he's doing" or "Those two are mine, and—oh, him? He's just a foster kid."

When people say these things, they have no idea how much it hurts the person they're speaking about. The term *foster child* itself, if said in a certain way, becomes a put-down.

Walking around the halls of my school, I hear the jokes of my classmates. Things like: "Group home kid" (in reference to someone who acts up in class) and "You delinquent" (in reference to someone in care). Phrases used when speaking (most of the time) behind our backs.

One memory that stands out the most is when I overheard a girl talking about her foster sister in the school lunchroom.

"Yeah, and that little b-tch dared to talk to my mother that way. Is it my mother's fault that her father molested her? Was it my mother's fault he beat her too? Why should that little delinquent get the same as the rest of us? We are my mother's real children, not her. She probably liked her father molesting her, that little group-home slut."

My friends who knew I was in foster care looked at the girl, then looked at me, and waited to see what I was going to say. They were as shocked as I was.

I looked across the table at her and anger swelled in me. How could she say such a thing? How could she speak that way about some-one else's personal life? I could see that she hated her foster sister bit-terly. How could she let herself be so limited and narrow-minded in her thinking?

I wondered what kind of family could allow such hate toward a family member. And I knew that I had never, in all my years in fos-ter care, met a person so bent on cruelty toward another.

I could nearly taste the acid in my stomach. Harsh words filled my head as I looked at the girl, but I didn't say them. Instead, with-out so much as a word or a second look, I stood up and left the table.

Before that moment, I used to envy the "normal" people who were given the chance to live with their own blood. But after that day, when I saw the hate that came from a "normal" family's life, I looked at my own world and was content.

❏

Marcus J. Howell, 17, lived in foster care for most of his child-hood. He left the system in 1994 to return to his father. He says his "biggest strength" is being able to "remember the emotions of my childhood and to try to understand them." He wants to be a chef and a writer.

SHORT TAKES: WHO WILL I BECOME?

NO WAY OUT

Max Morán, *18, Staten Island, N.Y.*

H ere I am chilling on the last car of a Brooklyn-bound train. Don't ask me how, but I always end up all the way back here. I'm dressed as if I'm ready for war. This is what I do when I want to get away from reality. I ride the trains all night long.

Now I close my eyes and travel to a good place, a place where life is worth living. No crime, no rapes, no sound of gunshots, and no discrimination. A place so far away from here that it is hard to imagine.

People I know be saying there's no way out from the streets, but I will find a way. I'm not ashamed of where I'm from, but I'm tired of this ghetto world. Even where I live in Staten Island there are so many clowns acting wild.

A couple of years ago a kid was shot and killed on my block. Why? Because he was staring at the murderer. Staring is a fool's game, yet sometimes I can be the biggest fool when I'm stressed out, which basically is every day.

My new roommate has a gun in our room and yesterday we got into a big argument. Then he gave me that speech: "You better chill, you don't know where I'm from." I laughed at him and told him that real men don't need guns.

When I lived in the Bronx, I grew up with kids who always carried guns. One of my friends is dead and the other is doing time for a stick-up. I don't want to end up like that. I know better.

This is my senior year in high school and I'm feeling the pressure. I got two choices: a dead-end job or college. I can't picture myself in school in the future, but I don't want to keep on making five dollars an hour from nine to five and feeling like a slave.

I'm worth more than five dollars and I'm too proud to beg for quarters. I'm an intelligent young Hispanic male who will never commit a crime because my mind is too precious to be trapped in a dark cell.

I got so many things on my mind that I can't even get in the Christmas spirit. I really don't have to, because I celebrate Christmas every day by showing love to those who care for and respect me. My love is worth much more than some stupid presents.

Wow! There's a cutie sitting across from me, let me smile at her. Oh! She smiled back. Should I talk to her? No, let's just continue with my journey.

At times like this I wish I wasn't so shy, but the past has taught me how easy it is to fall in love with a pretty face. Then again, she could look much prettier if she wasn't dressed like me.

Today's world got me bugging, I don't understand why we guys call girls b-tches. When I become a father, I surely won't want anybody calling my little girl a b-tch. Even when a girl disses me, I refuse to call her that.

Just last week this girl played me out lovely. We knew each other for three months and it was all good. Then things started to get serious and she wanted to know more about me.

She told me that she liked me, but her parents wouldn't approve of me because I live in a group home. I told her my living situation doesn't matter—if she likes me, forget her parents. I mean, I was interested in her, not her parents.

But I realized I was in a no-win situation. I simply smiled at her and wished her a good life. It's her loss because I got mad love to give.

Well, by the next stop I'll be in Coney Island. I'm going to sit under the boardwalk and listen to the ocean, feeling the cold air that sends chills up my spine.

I'm thinking about a couple of friends who are getting caught up in the drug game. Sometimes it brings tears to my eyes.

It is so quiet here, no phone ringing, no beepers beeping, nobody screaming out my name. People be saying that I be acting like I'm all that, just because I don't say much and keep things to myself. Just because I'm shy, that doesn't mean I like being alone. I always have been misunderstood.

I'm going to sit here for a while and hopefully I will not fall asleep like I did the last time. This time I will try to reach a star and also look at the moon, imagining that bright powder falling off. I guess I'm going crazy and things I be thinking about make me scared. At times like this I could do anything for a kiss or a hug, yet I only like giving a pound to those whose hearts are in their hands.

Great! This girl beeped me again. If I didn't call her the first time, what makes her think I will do it now? Back in the days I used to have a beeper for all the wrong reasons.

I'm simply tired of this world, where a typical criminal description fits me almost perfectly. Christmas and birthdays have missed me for the last eight years, no family to talk about, so don't ask me why I'm depressed all the time. As I sit here, I can put everything in perspective.

Today I will watch the sunrise. But I never want the sun to set on me. I'm too young, I need the warmth of the sun. Only eighteen, but I'm running out of time. I will leave the streets behind me. Come and follow me if you want, but if you don't, I won't think any less of you. In this life only the strong survive, and I've survived long enough.

THE WAY I WAS RAISED

Anonymous, *15, Brooklyn, N.Y.*

If there was one thing I could change about my past, it would be the way I was raised.

I was adopted at the age of six months from Colombia by a white family. I felt very uneasy being a Latino in a white family. The first couple of years were okay, but then I started messing up. I would do things, such as take gum and stick it on the side of the dresser. I was young and didn't know any better, but instead of my family talking to me and explaining how I was wrong, they would label me.

When I say label, I mean they would call me a troublemaker or something like that, and I would get a beating. A beating to them didn't mean just taking a belt and hitting my behind a couple of times. To them it meant smacking me in the face and mentally punishing me. For instance, they would yell and scream that I wasn't a part of their family.

I was raised not to know who my biological family was, and to be prejudiced against black people. Even though I eventually learned not to be prejudiced, I still don't know who my real family is. In general, I was raised to be something I'm not . . . white.

If I could change the way I was raised, I would make it so that my adoptive parents told me who my real family was and didn't use their hands to show me that I was wrong in expressing myself the way I did. I would also make it so that somebody showed me that they loved me.

A HEART THAT LOVES

Dhanisha Jarecha, *18, Elizabeth, N.J.*

Once, when I used to live in India, I met this girl named Bhakti. In time, we became the best of friends. But when we first met, I always wondered why she would talk to me because I wasn't pretty at all, and she was the prettiest girl I had ever seen.

One day, after we got to know each other, I asked her, "Why do you talk to me? I'm not that pretty." She looked at me, smiled, and told me that I was very beautiful, and what makes a person beautiful is their heart, soul, and conscience. A person can be the most beautiful person alive on the outside, but if their heart doesn't have love, kindness, understanding, and gentleness, that person cannot be beautiful. There is no way they can be beautiful without the soul and conscience that tells right from wrong.

Until this day I remember her words, and I also remember that she is the only person in my life, besides my foster family, who judged me from the inside, not the outside.

WHY NOT ME?

Zerlena Ronda, *17, Johnstown, N.Y.*

Every time I get restricted and every time I can't get along with another girl, I always say, *"Why me?"* I hate hearing myself saying that stupid line over and over again.

When I was living at home I always got a lot of abuse, so I didn't have many friends, I got low grades, and I hated myself.

After I got placed into placement voluntarily because of my mother's behavior, I really became a depression case. I always let other girls pick on me and make me feel like nothing. I then began to do everything for everyone so that they wouldn't be mean, so that I could go to sleep at night without having to worry if I would get beat up or if all of the few things that I had would be stolen.

I was soon the dog of the dorm. I would help the girls with everything. But when they were in a bad mood, I would get the bad end of the stick.

I was at the point where I couldn't do it anymore. I ran away from the placement that I was in. I ran around the block and went to the store. When I got there I called my mother and she called the cops and I was soon arrested.

I was brought back and put in a room for four days. While in solitary confinement I talked to my staff. She made me realize that placement is where you get away from all of the abuse and where you try to work on all of the things that can make your life better after you deal with them. She said placement is what you make of it.

I came out of that room a new person. All this time I had been wondering, *Why me? Why not me?*

I worked really hard and I didn't take crap from anyone. I was gaining respect where and when I needed it. I never gave any of the new girls the hassle and pain that I got. I did really good in that placement and after two years I got put into a group home.

I have been in this group home for almost two years and I am more successful than I ever thought I would be in my whole entire life. I am a published poet, I have a lot of friends, I am respected, and I like myself. I am seventeen and I am going into the eleventh grade. I also have a job and I am planning to go to college in the near future.

Living in placement has been tough at times, but it has also been for the best. All of the best and important memories of my life have been in placement. So when times are getting you to the point of giving up, just remember, anyone can do it if they try. And don't ever forget, *Why* not *me?*

IV
LOOKING TO THE
FUTURE

CHANGE

Yo, look Tanya, what cee?
There goes Kenyetta,
but it's not Kenyetta.

That's not the Kenyetta
who used to live
at 1071 Franklin Ave.
in the Bronx.

That's not the Kenyetta
who did not care
about her own life.

That's not the Kenyetta
who used to cut school
with her so-called friends.

That's not the Kenyetta
who used to fight
all the time.

She is not the one
who used to smoke weed
or drink, who
was always asking
for a C.I.

That can't be the one
who disrespected grownups,
even her parents.

It can't be, Tanya—
it's not, cee? It's the one
who stopped smoking
and drinking,
who asked others
to try and stop.

It's the one
who does not fight anymore,
or even think about it.

It's the one
who wants to go to college
and better herself,
and become a writer.

She is the one
who won't cut school for
    anybody,
the one you used to find
at the back of the class,
now at the head.

The one who has a better choice
in who she calls her friends.

She is the one who respects
    adults,
who asks her parents for
forgiveness.

The one who was on a bad
    path,
but now is on a good road.

The one we all wish
to see a lot more of—

—Kenyetta Ivy, 19

FROM FIGHTER TO FRIEND

Kenyetta Ivy

I came into the system in '92. It was in the summer. I remember the night I went to Laight Street, my first group home.

I arrived at 1:30 in the morning. When I entered the house I was scared, 'cause I always heard that people died in group homes. When I got inside, the girls were all sitting in the lounge. There were twenty-five girls in the house.

I stayed there for only a month, because I started hanging with the wrong crowd. I was smoking weed, drinking, and fighting. I was considered the baddest girl in the house. They had to get me out of there, so they moved me to another group home.

This one was called Coney Island Diagnostic. There were four girls living there. But I was kicked out 'cause I broke a girl's jaw. Me and the girl were screaming in the hall after the staff went to bed. The next day the girl told the staff it was my fault. I got in trouble for that, so I hit her. When I left for school the staff said don't come back, so I didn't.

I went to my grandmother's house and stayed there for two weeks. I was getting badder and badder. My friend's mother said I would be on "America's Most Wanted" at age sixteen. I told her, "Ha, I fooled you, I'm in a group home." I thought everything was a joke.

When I left my grandmother's house, I went to my old group

home, Sheltering Arms. My male friends paid me to get them girls they could have sex with. They called me a female pimp. I was asking myself, *How can I do this to another girl?* But I didn't care.

In October 1992, I went to court to get placed into another group home. It was a few days after my seventeenth birthday. They placed me in a thirty-day transitional center in Brooklyn.

This was a group home I fell in love with. I loved it so much 'cause all we did was smoke weed and have fun. I had a crew in there called BMP (Blunt Master Posse). We broke every rule in the book. I eventually had to leave because my thirty days were up.

This time they moved me to a lockdown in Queens. It was a coed group home, boys and girls. I went there with the intention of leaving. I was going to leave "By Any Means Necessary" so that's just what I did.

Me and the few friends I made in the three weeks I was there beat up this girl. The girl thought she was all that. My friends grabbed the girl outside the house. We beat her so bad she pressed charges.

When we got to the police station, they said I was going to jail. I was scared but I really didn't care. I stayed at the station for a few hours, then was let go. I went back to the group home. The next day I got moved again.

Moving from place to place was fun at first. By February of '93 I had been in eight group homes, picked up a tag name, and had over twenty fights. (My tag name was Bonnie, as in Bonnie and Clyde, the bank robbers.)

My last group home was back in the Bronx again. When I got there, I was wondering how long I would stay—a month, a week, a day, or at the rate I was going, an hour.

Staff seemed nice at first. Most of the time I stayed to myself, because the girls didn't come home until nighttime.

The coolest girl in the house was Kathy. I thought she was cool from the first time I met her because she was so quiet. But when I would start fights with the girls in the house, if they said something wrong to me, Kathy would jump right in.

The staff in the house said that Kathy acted like my mother or something. She would always get me out of trouble. I still fought, but I was starting to slow down. See, every time I got into a fight, Kathy would take me for a walk.

Kathy was the only one who ever (I mean ever since I was born) encouraged me to make something of myself. She told me fighting was not the move. I looked at her as a mother figure, because she treated me like she really cared and I knew she did.

I always thought the people I hung out with cared, but I was wrong. Kathy said that if they cared for you, they wouldn't tell you to do bad things, such as smoking and stuff, but the right things. I knew she was right, because when I followed her advice I always had a positive outcome.

Kathy and I were hanging out more and more. After a while I started calling her my best friend. The staff became jealous, because at one point Kathy had been close to them. She used to tell them her problems, but now she was confiding in me.

Staff started calling me sneaky and told the other residents not to trust me. Kathy said, "Bonnie, you're not sneaky, they just don't understand you."

In the system, residents understand other residents 'cause they have almost the same problems. Staff thinks and looks at it another way. So they put us down mentally, emotionally, sometimes physically. Kathy said that I just needed someone to care for me.

She always told me it was positive over negative, and that if you respect a person, you will get the same respect back. I became a positive person. I was given a single room. When I first arrived I was on restriction every day, and now I was never on restriction.

It came to the point that when I saw a fight, I would try to break it up. I never knew a person could change someone that much, but Kathy changed me. She gave me a heart I could not get anywhere else. I think that if I hadn't met Kathy, I would still be listening to those people who call themselves my "friends."

Me and Kathy made big plans to go to college and then into the health field. I stayed in my room and wrote poems while she practiced dancing.

We were chosen to see Mayor Dinkins for a special discussion on youth. (Back in the days, the only person I thought I would be chosen to see was the judge.)

Every night before I went to bed, I would thank God for a friend like her. Now I think that wasn't enough.

One day me and Kathy got into a fight because I called her a b-tch. I was only playing, but she took it the wrong way. We got into a verbal fight. I got mad and said a lot of things that hurt her.

She always told me you can't break up a true friendship, but I now realize that you can after I felt the pain of losing a friend.

I miss Kathy and still love her dearly. After a while I gave up on getting our friendship back, 'cause I kept trying and it wasn't working.

Now I'm still on the right track and still thinking of the advice she gave me. I thank God for the good times as well as the bad. Although we are no longer friends, I just don't know where I would be without her.

I know if God wants it, we will be friends again, and I hope that day is soon.

❏

Kenyetta Ivy, 17, wrote this story in the fall of 1992. A winner of several scholarships and awards for participation in civic affairs, she is now attending Mohawk Valley Community College in upstate New York. Kenyetta plans to complete her education at a four-year college and major in journalism.

STAYING
WITH THE HURT

Tasheen Davis

S oon after my daughter Anasia was born, her father went off to jail for sticking up a man for his money. So I had to convince myself that I was going to be the happiest single parent there ever was.

I told myself that I was going to give my child everything that she needed and wanted (being that I was only seventeen years old, I had no choice but to think that way).

I also told myself that I was never going to hit my child, because I didn't want her to experience the same kind of abuse that I took from my own father when I was pregnant with her.

I was going to start a new life with a new person in a Mother and Infant Program, a place for young teenage mothers who have no home. But as I started my new life, I found myself putting off everything I had been saying about the way I would treat my daughter.

Anasia was one and a half months old when I hit her for the first time. I hit her because she kept crying for no reason and I thought hitting her would make her stop.

When Anasia turned two months old, the hitting increased and I also started screaming at her.

And when she was three months old, Anasia fell off her high-rise bed. She was crying and crying, and I left her on the floor to cry. I didn't pick her up until I was ready to get out of my own bed.

I kept asking myself, *Why do I keep hitting her?* I didn't know if I was hitting her because her father wasn't around or because I couldn't face being a teenage mother.

(Now, as I look back on the past, I know the reason. It was my first time being in foster care, and I never had to deal with any rules and regulations before. Dealing with the rules made me stress out.)

When Anasia was nine or ten months old, she had a seizure in my arms. I didn't know if it was because I was hitting her too much or because I wasn't feeding her enough. (To tell you the truth, I really didn't give a damn what it was from.) Half of me wanted to hurry up and take her to the hospital, and the other half was saying, *No, don't take her, let her die because you don't want her.*

While I was taking my time to decide what to do, I was looking at this person in my arms. Her eye was closed up, her lips were blue from not getting enough air, and her body was shaking. I finally made up my mind to take her to the hospital and leave her there, so that's what I did.

The doctors rushed Anasia out of my arms and took her to another room. I stood in the emergency room for about five or ten minutes, then I turned around and walked away. As I did, I heard Anasia start to cry, but I tried to pay it no mind. Then she started to cry even louder and the people in the emergency room were looking at me in a funny way.

So I couldn't help but turn around and go into the hospital to see what was wrong with her. But I was just pretending, so I could make myself look like a good and concerned mother.

As I entered the room she was in, Anasia had lots of I.V. tubes in her arms and legs and an oxygen mask over her face. Her eyes were so big. It seemed as if she was telling me to help her, with little tears in the corners of her eyes. I couldn't help but cry and ask myself, *Why?* I knew that I needed help.

I joined a group of teenagers called the Mentor's Group at an agency called Rosalie Hall, in the Bronx. They get together to discuss problems they're having and how to find ways to deal with them.

When I joined the Mentor's Group, I was afraid to tell them about the abuse I had done to my child. I don't know why, but as I started to listen to the stories that everyone was sharing with each other, I felt relieved and started opening up to them. Some of the things they were talking about I could relate to, such as being a single parent and raising a child in the system.

Then I caught myself and realized that nobody was sharing anything similar to what I had done to Anasia, so I felt that the group was not for me. But a girl shared her experience of being abused mentally and physically (by either her mother or father, I can't remember), and after listening to her story, I couldn't help but to open up and tell them about what I had done to Anasia.

After I told my story, the group was quiet and didn't say anything at first. I thought they wouldn't understand me and were going to hate me, but I was wrong. They were quiet because of the abuse that I had done to my child, but also because they were trying to think of a way to help and support me in the best way they could.

The first thing they told me was that I had to stay with the hurt and not the anger. In other words, they were trying to say that if I was angry at my baby's father for leaving me, or if I was angry for being a mother at such a young age, I shouldn't take it out on Anasia. She didn't ask to be here, she didn't ask for anybody to hit or hate her, only to love her and show her the right way in life.

Listening to them made me feel so low about myself, because what they said was so powerful and so true. I had to accept the fact that Anasia was not the reason for my anger and should not be the target of it. That's a message that I've kept near to my heart, and it's made me become a better person. (Thanks, guys.)

Now that Anasia is fifteen months, she's getting into things, but I don't get the urge to hit or scream at her anymore. I try my best to put all the hitting and screaming behind us both. I try to make up for the past by taking her to the park, playing pitty-pat, reading books at night, and showing Anasia her eyes, nose, mouth, and ears, and telling her what they are used for.

If there was something that I could say to my daughter, it would be this: Anasia, there is a God and He didn't let those foster people take you away from me. I believe in my heart that He's giving me a second chance to prove to you and to myself how much I love and appreciate you.

Love you, 'Nasia!

❏

Since writing this article, Tasheen Davis, 18, has left foster care and now lives in the Bronx with her daughter. She recently earned her high school equivalency diploma and is enrolled in a business school. "My relationship with Anasia is much closer and stronger than it ever was," she says, "and I feel more like a mother than I did before."

MY FAMILY SECRET

Tieysha McVay

I was sexually abused as a young child. My abuser was a close family friend, and he is only six years older than me.

The first attack happened when I was only four years old. My grandmother was babysitting me and that's when the abuse started.

My abuser (I'll call him Jay) had come by to visit after church. I was in the living room playing with my Barbie doll when he approached me. He asked me if I knew where babies come from, and then he pushed my Barbie doll between my legs. I screamed, and he stopped when my grandmother (who was in the kitchen) asked what was wrong. But the abuse didn't end there.

The next time I remember I was seven years old. My mother, who was going to school and working overtime, was sleeping in her bedroom. Jay popped up at my house that day.

I was watching television and playing with my toys as he entered my room. Jay became very aggressive and started cursing. The next thing I realized he pushed me down on my bed, tugged at my clothes (until they were off) while spitting at me, slapping me, threatening me, and telling me to shut up.

I tried to push him off me by kicking, scratching, biting, and yelling, but he managed to penetrate me anyway. The attack lasted about fifteen or twenty minutes.

When Jay finished, he started laughing like the whole thing was funny. I cried out loud, feeling ashamed, scared, and dirty. My mother was awakened by the noise and from her bedroom asked what was going on. I did not know what to say, so I said, "Everything is all right, we were just fighting over my toys."

(I guess being so active with her studies and work, my mother didn't feel like getting out of bed to see what was really the matter.)

I clearly remember that day, that fatal sexual experience. It was definitely a surprise, because Jay was not a bad teenager.

Jay's father and mother lived in our neighborhood. His older sister and my mother went to school together. Jay went to church every Sunday, and hung out with my older cousins. So I didn't understand why he would want to hurt me.

Going back to the attacks, they usually took place after his church services were over on Sundays. I dreaded that day, knowing what was going to happen. Even though I didn't want those awful things to happen to me, they did anyway.

In the beginning I thought the abuse was normal. I was only a child! Sometimes Jay, along with my older cousin, would be asked to watch me so the adults could go grocery shopping, to the hair salon, car repair shop, etc.

I was told that it was all right to give Jay a hug or a kiss on the cheek, that it was okay for him to supervise me while I was taking a bath. After all, Jay was just like one of my relatives.

About two years into the abuse, someone else in my family found out. It was a Saturday afternoon and my mother was giving a Tupperware party. The house was filled with a bunch of people. My cousin Lee, Jay, and I started playing some records and bugging out, telling jokes like teenagers do. Then Jay decided he wanted to hurt me.

Lee was right there. He watched as Jay fondled my breasts, touched me between my legs, and tried to get my clothes off. Lee didn't even try to stop him. Again I started to cry, fighting back, but it kept going on.

Finally the monster left the house. I was alone with Lee. He teased me, saying that he would tell my mother and everyone at the party. I tugged at his arm, begging him not to tell, and promising him I'd give him my allowance or cover for him when he came home late. Lee said he wouldn't tell and he kept his mouth shut.

The sexual abuse lasted for five years. I was too ashamed to tell anyone. I thought either I would be blamed for the abuse, or no one would believe me. And I thought it happened to me because I had done something bad.

Jay used verbal and physical threats to keep me in line so I wouldn't tell on him. He would slap me when I started to cry, and tell me he'd do it again much harder if I didn't shut up. Often times he would pull out knives on me and threaten to hurt me, so I kept quiet and did as I was told.

The last attack took place in October 1986. It had been a very busy day in my household. I was home alone sleeping in bed. Jay called (it was 8:00 in the morning) and asked me if my mother was home. I said no, he hung up, and the next thing I realized he was ringing my doorbell.

Just as I was about to open the door to tell him to leave, my grandmother pulled up in her car. She let him in, but told him he couldn't stay. Her instructions were for him to take the trash out and go home, but instead Jay hid in the basement.

My grandmother called me downstairs to ask if there was anything I wanted and to inform me that she would be gone for a little while. I said "No, thanks" and went back upstairs.

When I came back up to my room Jay was standing in front of me. I realized he had been in my mother's bedroom. Her diamond engagement ring was on my dresser. Jay was planning on stealing it. He was talking to me, but I didn't hear him. I was concentrating on the ring. That's when he threw me on the bed and tried to force my clothes off to abuse me.

I was mighty strong that day. I managed to kick him in the groin and hurt him. I jumped up to run downstairs, but he caught me, pulled out a knife, and said, "I'm gonna f-ck you up, you little b-tch."

I quickly grabbed the knife from him, struck him in the leg, and ran. I was crying by the time I reached my grandmother, who hadn't left the house yet. I blurted out enough to let her know Jay was upstairs. He came down and she asked him what he was still doing in the house. Jay was bleeding and that's when she realized something bad had happened.

Jay left the house. I stopped crying and told my grandmother what happened. She looked at me in amazement and asked, "What happened? Did Jay touch you? How long was he upstairs?"

I really couldn't speak. I just cried and stood in the middle of the kitchen, shaking my head.

That night I told the same story to Jay's parents and other relatives of mine and they all had the same nonchalant attitude. Like nothing had actually happened. But I knew what had happened and I left it at that.

It wasn't until I came into the foster care system that my relatives learned all the untold secrets of the abuse. Before that, they knew only of the final attack.

Once in the system, I learned that many of the young girls in placement had gone through some of the same experiences as I did in my early childhood.

One night while preparing to go to bed, we got into a deep conversation about why we were in placement. The subject of being sexually abused came to the surface. From that point on we occasionally talked about our situations. Two months later, a boy from the other side of our placement sneaked into our cottage and fondled some of the girls. (I was included!)

There were meetings held to get our reactions and concerns about what happened. During the meeting some of the girls spoke out and said that it wasn't the first time something like that had happened to them. At that point I knew I was not alone. A bunch of us decided to get some therapy to help ourselves heal the pain. A student social worker helped us find a support group for those who have been raped or molested. I went with the girls from my placement for comfort, security, and familiarity.

It was terribly scary in the beginning when we attended. There was lots of crying from the other members. Although we could identify with their emotions, we held back about our personal situations. We didn't speak to the group about our problems until after the fifth visit.

We participated in group therapy for three months until our worker had to leave and return to school. It helped us a bit to deal with the past. It didn't take away what happened, but it was a healthy start to recovery. It worked out well because we knew we needed to seek help to feel better.

I thought I was over my tragic experience until I became a high school student and started to date guys.

Until then, I didn't realize how much emotional and mental damage had been done to my life. The results began to appear when I dated a man or just hung out with some of my male acquaintances.

Every male I dated wanted the same thing. That is, to get into the female's pants. I was very fragile after what happened to me in the past. I would act strangely with some of them, even the ones who didn't seem interested in sex. Most of them got cut off before I found out what kind of relationship they wanted.

Later that year, when I discussed my situation with a social worker, she said it was probably because I had been abused as a child. She wasted no time and got me an individual therapist to talk to. I was in session with my therapist for a year and a half.

She really was good at bringing out the pain. She took her time explaining things to me and always assured me being abused was not my fault. She also told me it was very helpful to cry when there wasn't anyone to talk to. I felt a little better about myself. Over time, my intimate relationships have gotten easier to deal with. I know that my experience is only for me to know. I don't have to explain to every man I date what happened to me. My therapist told me I don't even have to tell my husband if I don't want to.

But to this day, relatives place guilt on me for what occurred. I often wonder: do they really understand what I went through back then and what I feel to this day?

Their attitudes are like, "So what? We don't really believe he did that, the whole story is a lie, we don't care what happened to you in the past. Jay's parents and our family have been close for so many years, we're not going to stop being friends 'cause of your problems."

My grandmother even accused me of wanting Jay to rape and abuse me! She said if I got hurt, I had it coming because I was a "problem child." And she warned me that some man might want to hurt me again.

I really get upset when my family reacts like that. What reason have I ever given anyone to hurt me verbally or physically? I never asked to be a victim of sexual abuse and they make me feel totally alone in dealing with the past.

My therapist advised me to ignore the brutal comments my relatives make and constantly reminded me I wasn't alone and that in time I would learn to be comfortable in all relationships.

As for Jay, he never got punished for what he did to me, but he did get caught for selling drugs and robbery, and went to prison. Although it didn't have anything to do with me, he got exactly what was coming to him, and I am glad he did.

There are many ways I am reminded about the abuse—by newspaper reports, close friends telling me their stories, or the way a present boyfriend might talk to me or touch me.

Once this guy came to take me out on a date. I freaked out and didn't want to get into his car. I believe I had this reaction because I didn't know what his expectations were for our date, and the situation overwhelmed me.

A week later we decided to try another date. I was nervous, but went along with our plans. We went to the movies and, as we were going up the escalator, he put his arms around me. I tried to push his hands away and he said: "Don't push me away. Just relax and everything will be all right."

I was reminded of my abuse, because those were the words Jay would often use. I wanted badly to escape from his grip and end the date. But I calmed myself and realized he didn't want to hurt me. He only wanted to be affectionate. The date continued and so did our relationship. We dated for over a year.

So you see, sexual abuse has had a big impact on my life, but I am gradually learning to trust again and to have hope for the future.

❏

Tieysha McVay, 21, had been in foster care for nine years when she wrote this story. "So many kids have a hard time dealing with their problems," she writes, "that they fail to realize the positive side to living in foster care. It's not all bad and the system can really help them improve and achieve in the future." Tieysha is studying to be a nurse at Kingsborough Community College in Brooklyn.

THERAPY
CHANGED MY LIFE

Lenny Jones

T herapy helped me let out a lot of anger I had locked inside. It changed my life, and it could change your life. It helped me to better myself.

My father, whose name is Ron, used to beat me a lot for no reason at all (he was drunk about 99.9 percent of the time). He used to make me and my older brother Kevin go to the store and buy him beer and condoms. He sent us for condoms because he would have several females coming to the house (not all at once). My father didn't care what time of day it was, he would make us run errands for him. I was only a young kid when I was being sent on errands.

As I got older, things got worse. One day my father went out and left me with one of his co-workers named Tracy. I never knew why my father did this.

Tracy and I were in the living room watching TV and Tracy asked me if anybody was in the back room. I said no. I didn't think anything else about it.

Tracy went in the back room and called me. I went in the back room. Tracy was sitting on one of the beds. Tracy called me over, so I went.

Next thing I knew, Tracy unzipped my pants and pulled them down. I was only six and I was very afraid. Then Tracy pulled down my underwear. Tracy told me to lay down on the bed, so I did.

Tracy did the same thing I was told to do. Then Tracy lay down on the bed and forced me to have oral sex.

Later that night when it was all over, my brother Kevin came home and I told him what happened. My brother took me to a friend of my father's named Macho because he didn't know where my father was and he trusted Macho.

Macho, who lived right around the corner, at first had mixed feelings when he heard what happened. He had known Tracy for so long that he couldn't believe Tracy would do such a thing. On the other hand, Macho trusted me and knew that I wouldn't lie to him.

I didn't know it, but Tracy had followed Kevin and me to Macho's house. When Tracy came in, Macho took his cane and started hitting Tracy until Tracy was just about unconscious. Then Macho's wife called the cops.

The next thing I knew I was in the police station with my father and brother. I remember telling lots of cops and a therapist what happened. I remember having to demonstrate in front of some people with two dolls.

I also remember the expression on my father's face when he and I were alone. It looked like he was upset, but not because of what Tracy did. Instead, it looked like he was mad at me for making him go through all this trouble. It was like I could read my father's mind, which said, "Damn! Why did you have to put me through all this bullsh-t?"

I went back home. I don't know if charges were ever pressed against Tracy. There was one good thing that came out of my ordeal— I never saw Tracy again.

As I got older, my life with my father got worse. For a while he had stopped abusing me and Kevin, but after his girlfriend was killed in a car accident he started drinking, gambling, and abusing us mentally, physically, and verbally all over again. My aunt Maroline decided to send me to my cousin's house when she found out what was going on.

But my cousin contributed to my problems by verbally and physically abusing me. I was thinking of running away, but I didn't know how.

One day when I was in the library I saw a book called *I Hate School*. In the back of the book I saw the phone number for Covenant House. I called and made arrangements to go there the following day.

The next day I put on three pairs of socks, two pairs of pants, two shirts, and my flight jacket. In my book bag I had clothes instead of books. My cousin had no idea what I was doing because I packed my bag behind her back. When I stepped out the door I was very happy, because I felt I was leaving hell and going to heaven.

When I went to Covenant House, I was a little shaky about telling perfect strangers my problems, telling them things I had never told anyone else before.

While I was there I had to see a therapist. It was mandatory. I was in the waiting area for quite a while. Then I heard my name called.

The therapist's name was Dr. Smith. I told Dr. Smith how my father abused me, and how I ended up living with my abusive cousin. And when I spoke about how I was abused sexually, mentally, verbally, and spiritually, I cried, and Dr. Smith would, too. That's when I realized that she was there to help me and not to hurt me.

Dr. Smith gained my trust in many different ways. One way she gained my trust was when my caseworker was going to send me back to my cousin's house. Dr. Smith fought to keep me from going back because she believed I was telling the truth.

Another way she gained my trust was when I got dumped by a girl I really cared about and was on the brink of suicide. I was standing on the sidewalk crying. Dr. Smith was going to her car, about to go home, when she saw me shivering.

She came over and asked me what was wrong and I said nothing. She knew something was wrong, so she walked me to her office. After about ten minutes of silence I finally told her. The conversation wasn't over until an hour and a half later.

After that, I felt like I was floating on air. I trusted Dr. Smith more than ever because she worked overtime and without pay just to help me with my problem. If I went to my father with a problem like that, he'd probably laugh in my face and walk away.

From then on I felt that it wasn't just a therapist-client kind of thing. I felt it was a friendship and that we had an understanding with one another.

I had so much anger locked in for so long it almost drove me crazy. Every time I told my story to other counselors at Covenant House, I would add a little more because I was feeling more and more comfortable talking to people about my situation.

After a month or so I was placed in a group home in Queens. It was much more peaceful because it was on beachfront property. Whenever I was upset and didn't feel like talking to anyone, I would go out on the beach, sit down on the sand, and let the roar of the ocean tides cause my anger to drift away.

I didn't feel comfortable around the group home therapist. The group home therapist was a male. I felt more comfortable talking to a female about my problems, because Dr. Smith was like the mother I never had.

I stopped going to the group home therapist after the first session because somehow he found out that I was a pyromaniac (a person who sets fires). Dr. Smith had told me I set fires out of anger.

The group home therapist seemed more aggressive and more in a rush than Dr. Smith. He didn't make me feel comfortable. All he did was ask me the same questions *("Do you fantasize about fire? Do you dream about fire? Are there voices in your head telling you to start fires?")* twenty times in one minute (which annoyed the hell out of me). When he asked me if I wanted to talk about anything else (he did all the talking), I said no and left.

Finding a therapist who is right for you isn't always easy, but if you do find one that is right for you, don't let 'em go. If Dr. Smith was the therapist for my group home, I'd still be going to therapy. I still keep in contact with her because she's my best friend. From sessions with Dr. Smith, I learned that you don't have to be crazy to see a psychiatrist.

Even after therapy, I sometimes feel guilty and depressed. I wonder if, by running away from my cousin's house, I hurt my aunt who had me moved there. (My aunt says she still loves me.)

As for my brother Kevin, he has always stood by me. He never wanted anything to happen to me. But Kevin doesn't want to deal with his anger. Once, I told Kevin about the abuse at my cousin's house. Kevin said, "Is she feeding you? Is she giving you clothes?" I said yes, but she wasn't doing enough positive things to cover up the negative things that she was doing to me. Kevin never really wanted to hear about the negative. I didn't know why. We're different that way. I feel it's always better to look at a problem directly.

For example, Kevin still loves my father, even after all the stuff he put him through. Kevin is trying to cover up his feelings, but I don't think he should. I think that's why Kevin catches a temper sometimes (much quicker than I do).

You can't criticize Kevin about one thing, even if it's constructive. I think Kevin should go to therapy like I did, because even though he's twenty and I'm sixteen, I'm more mature because I know how to control my anger by expressing it. I don't pretend everything's all right.

I still have a temper that I occasionally let out, mostly to counselors, sometimes to residents. But I'm much better at dealing with it than I was before.

If you have problems, don't keep them locked in or they will affect your life more than you think. If you keep your anger locked in, you might end up abusing your kids. Then they will either continue the cycle of abuse or run away from home like I did.

❏

Lenny Jones, 16, began writing this story in the third person before shifting into the first person. It was originally published anonymously, but Lenny decided to put his name on it in this book because "it was a difficult story that took many drafts over a period of months, but once it was published, I felt a weight off my shoulders and that I could talk about the experience more openly without hiding my identity."

HOW I MADE PEACE
WITH THE PAST

Paula Byrd

I remember the sadness in my mother's eyes as we sat in her hospital room, watching her deteriorate as the days went by. She had been in and out of the hospital for months, due to her illness and her misuse of drugs. My mother had AIDS, the disease that affects your immune system.

Since she was hospitalized in January, my youngest brother Tyrone and I had not been able to go to see her at first. My mother had to have an operation. We couldn't go see her until she was able to speak.

But as soon as she was better, we went to see her. As we were coming to my mother's room, all of a sudden my heart just starting beating real heavy. I thought it was going to stop right there. I was so scared because I didn't know what to expect.

I had heard from my oldest brother William that she was getting worse. We finally went in, and as I got closer and closer to her bed, tears just started rolling down my face. I couldn't believe that this small woman who was laying in the bed was my mother.

She had lost way too much weight. I wanted to hug her but was too afraid of hurting her, so I didn't. I just said hello. You could hear in her voice that she was very sick and weak. It seemed as if she knew her time was coming.

She had gotten so sick that she wasn't able to move or get out of bed. She couldn't use the bathroom, so she was put on Pampers. I did not like the sight of my mother laying in bed powerless, unable to function. I tried to have a conversation with her.

"Hi, Ma. Are you all right? Is the hospital treating you good? Are you eating all your food?" (She didn't like the hospital food, so my brother brought her some whenever he could.)

But her only reply was, "Yes, ma'am." From that day forward, our names became *ma'am*.

You see, while my mother was in the hospital, the doctors found out she had a disease called dementia. (This is a deterioration or loss of mental faculties. It's similar to Alzheimer's disease that older people get.)

While my brother William was explaining her sickness to me and Tyrone, a tall lady entered the room. She introduced herself as Ms. Cynthia Allen, my mother's social worker. She started telling me and my brothers how it was so important that we come as often as we could, because they didn't know when my mother was going to leave this earth.

I wanted to scream as loud as I could to get out all the anger I was feeling. It was my first time seeing her since she went into the hospital.

I felt so confused because I tried to picture life without my mother, and I knew it would be hard because it would mean I wouldn't have a mother or a father.

I lost my father to AIDS and drugs also, back in 1987. Our mother was all we had and soon we would have to give her up, too. It was just too much to take in. But the most difficult thing I had to deal with as a female was that I wouldn't have a mother anymore.

I remembered all those times I would cry myself to sleep, because I missed her very much, and I knew she was going to die. But I always thought that the people who did the research on AIDS would soon find a cure.

It was hurtful to know that soon she would no longer be there for me, because we were just beginning to build up our relationship again. Me and my brothers had to grow up fast for our ages. (I'm eighteen, Tyrone is seventeen, and William is twenty.)

We also have a new addition to our family, Lethia, who's five years old. She also has HIV.

Lethia was infected in the womb. When my mother first found

out that my sister had the disease, she gave Lethia up for adoption. My sister is very well aware of her sickness, she's very healthy, and she takes her own medication daily.

There was a time when I was so mad at my mother for not being there for us that I stopped going on home visits and kept myself isolated from her. I was very bitter that my mother transmitted HIV to my sister because she had unprotected sex. I kept remembering how she used to always tell me how important it was to never have sex without a condom, because you could be at risk to get something, and then she went and did the opposite.

But then my ways of thinking started to change after she went into the hospital in January. I had to learn to forgive her mistakes and accept what happened to my mother and my sister. It was a terrible accident that my mother wouldn't have made had she not been taken over by drugs.

Her one-night stand for money cost my mother her kids, her health, and even her life. But what was done was now over. I had to overcome all that and learn to communicate with her. After all, she was still my mother, no matter what.

So slowly I began to build up a relationship with her. However, my first step in doing that was to let her know how she hurt me. I had to express my anger and how I felt to her for the first time.

She did the one thing that no child should ever have to face. She chose her boyfriend over her own children. I explained to her that she was wrong because she was my mother, and no man should come between us.

Her only reply was that she was sorry for everything she did. I also told her that I hated all of her stealing and lying for money. I told her she should have been there for her children. A mother is supposed to help you, not hurt you.

She told me if she could take everything back she would, but she couldn't. She said she was truly sorry that she let her children down, but she would like to own up to her mistakes.

I told her that I knew she was sorry, but I couldn't hold in my anger toward her anymore. Expressing my feelings toward her enabled me to have faith in my mother again.

I will never forget, one day I went to the hospital to see her by myself. By then she had completely lost all her functions. She was unable to open her eyes or speak.

But somehow my mother knew I was there, because she shook

her head in response to what I was saying to her. I told her that I loved her and that I forgave her.

I also knew that deep down in my heart, she was sorry for everything she did in the past to me and my brothers, so all was forgiven and all grudges were put to rest.

I also told her that I would make something of myself, no matter what, and that we as a family would always stick together.

Those were the last words I ever got to say to my mother. She died on March 11, 1995. Although my mother has passed on, I feel a part of her lives on in my sister.

Lethia is well aware of what's going on. She's five and very smart for her age. I know there will come a time when Lethia will pass on too, but for now I take one day at a time.

I accept all the negative things that have happened and focus on the positive. For instance, making a better life for me and my brothers.

I spend as much time with my sister as I can. Don't get me wrong, I miss my parents very dearly, but I try to only think about the good times, because it helps me to cope better.

I put my faith in God. I pray that He will stand guard over my family and protect us from the negative influences out in the streets.

I strongly advise foster children who are going through what I have overcome to know the importance of letting your feelings out.

Because once that person is gone, they're not coming back. If there is something you need to say, say it even if the person hates the truth.

A lot of times you might feel that what happened to you is all right. You may feel that you shouldn't say anything, because the person who committed the acts has suffered enough.

Even if that's true, it is also important to let them know it wasn't all right and they hurt you. Even though you forgive them, you should get your anger off your chest.

It is important to let that person know how you feel when they are alive, so that when they do pass on, you won't feel like you've been cheated.

As for me and my family, my mother got a chance to hear we loved her. It wasn't because of guilt or because we knew she was going to die. It just was something we needed to say to her.

My point is, my mother got to hear how we felt about the whole situation before she was put to rest.

I wrote a poem that I'm sure everyone can relate to:

A FROZEN MIND

The shock of a sudden death
Makes some people feel
As if their minds are frozen.

This may be nature's way
Of protecting your mind,
So that everything can sink in
Slowly, and you won't be
Overwhelmed.

But if you talk to others and
Share your sadness,
Your mind will slowly begin to
defrost,
and you will start to adjust to your
loss.

Love Always,
Your Children

❏

Paula Byrd, 18, has been in foster care for eight years. She lives with her brother Tyrone in a foster home; her other brother, William, is now out of foster care. All three siblings visit regularly with their sister Lethia, who has been adopted. Paula recently received a Pinkerton Award Scholarship to attend Hunter College and wants to become a social worker "to make a difference in someone's life as well as my own." She adds, "Although I will age out soon, I will never forget what the foster care system has done for me and the lessons I learned in the process."

FACING THE PROBLEM

Eliott Castro

A bout a year ago I thought I was losing my mind. The girl I loved decided to break off with me. Today I don't blame her for leaving me, but at the time losing her hurt me a lot.

She broke off with me because I had a drinking problem, which she knew nothing about when she first met me, but which got worse during our relationship.

At the time I was living with my mother and I was being faced with verbal and sometimes physical abuse from her. I tried to bottle up my feelings by drowning them in alcohol. But this did no good, because I started verbally abusing my girlfriend, taking out on her the frustration and anger that my mother caused me.

Eventually we broke up and it gave me a perfect opportunity to continue my drinking. From that point on I just went buck wild crazy. I was completely destructive every time I drank. I'd end up kicking and punching through glass or walls until my fists would bleed. Then I would drink some more to forget whatever embarrassing stunt I had pulled in the last few minutes.

I was going through so much pain and hurt that hiding from my problems in alcohol only made them worse. Hiding from a problem never is the way to go about resolving it, no matter how harsh the problem might be or how hard it is to face it.

Everyone goes through problems and everyone has different

ways of dealing with them—reading a book, lifting weights, watching television, or staying away from others.

Now, what if I told you that these activities may not be the proper way of dealing with your problems? That watching TV or lifting weights can be as much of a problem as drinking?

I'm saying this because people often avoid the fact that they have a problem by doing something they enjoy or that relaxes them, so they can get their minds off the problem. I know, because that's exactly what I was doing. When I would sober up, the problem would be right there waiting for me. The fact that I was no longer with my girl only hurt more because I didn't want to deal with it.

The same thing applies when you pick up a book or go watch TV. When you're done keeping yourself occupied the problem is still going to be there, unless you decide to face it.

It isn't easy to admit to yourself or to anyone else that you have a problem, but it is necessary to do so in order to deal with it. Accepting the problem means looking at the trouble it is causing you and asking yourself: What can I do to relieve myself from it?

I had to start somewhere, so I began at home. I had no choice but to leave my mother because she was stopping me from reaching my goal of getting on with my life.

Now that I was completely alone, it was easier to go anywhere I chose. I stumbled upon this park in Brooklyn that faces the East River and there I started to evaluate myself. I chose this park because of its beauty.

The setting is quiet, there aren't many people there, and in front of you is the East River and the sun descending, which leaves a reflection of bright-colored lights on the water. Being there made it easier for me to look at myself and try to understand what I was doing wrong.

As the park relaxed my nerves, I started to look back on my life. Why was everything around me falling apart? What made me lose everything? Who was causing all of this to happen?

The only answer I could come up with was *me*. I realized that I had to make changes in my attitude and abnormal behavior. There was no one else to blame.

I evaluated why I needed to drink, why I was hurting, and what I was going to do to make things different. I realized that I drank because I felt sorry for myself. But I didn't really want to know what I was feeling sorry about, so I would drink some more.

The "why" was that I loved my girlfriend and losing her was

too painful to face. It hurt to think that I once had someone so good but lost her. What really made it painful was that I also drank to visualize her beside me. You might say I drank just to be with her again, sitting down next to me.

I also realized I was putting the weight of my problems totally on my shoulders. Which is why I had to take the next step.

That next step was hard. I realized that until I forgave myself, my problems wouldn't go away. I forgave myself for allowing the drinking to take over my life, I forgave myself for losing the girl I loved, and I forgave myself for the physical and mental damage I caused myself and others.

If I hadn't forgiven myself, I would have continued acting reckless. That was what I learned by sitting down and focusing my mind on solving my problems and not avoiding them.

Whatever it is you're going through, don't avoid your problems without getting some answers. Don't hide what you're going through—face it and make a change for the better.

Today I can deal with my problems and actually get things done by focusing on what I have to do. Of course, now and then I run into a little trouble, but I can handle it maturely, and I don't hold anything back by feeling sorry for myself.

Some of my thanks goes to that park in Brooklyn, but most of the credit goes to me.

❑

Eliott Castro, 18, has lived in several group homes and shelters for homeless teens.

A LONER
IN THE GROUP HOME

Mohamed Khan

T here was always a wall between me and other people, stopping me from speaking out or mingling with my peers. Unlike a normal kid my age, I never hung out with anyone. Come to think of it, I didn't even have one close friend. I'd go from school to my apartment, and that was all. But then I moved into a totally new world by going into a group home.

I used to live in East New York, Brooklyn. There were hardly any stores in my area and there weren't many people in the streets. My family's apartment was a small yet cozy place. There were four rooms and a bathroom for the five of us.

I went into the system in 1993 when I was fifteen. The group home that I entered was the total opposite of my family's apartment, in both size and neighborhood.

This new area was packed with people morning, noon, and night. This made me feel as if the whole world was crashing in on me. Everywhere I looked there were people. This would have been a good thing if I wasn't so obsessed with being alone. In addition, the group home was much bigger than my old apartment.

As I previously stated, I was a quiet kid before I went into the system. Many people knew me but never spoke to me, because I always had an air around me that said I wanted to be alone.

I wouldn't bother with the after-school ruckus involving sports or girl-watching. That wasn't my thing. Many days I preferred to just go home and do nothing. I would find comfort in not having to listen to anyone or try to impress anyone. I suppose I was a bit too self-conscious.

Then, in an instant, I was living with seven teenage boys and at least two supervisors. I knew for sure that I was no longer alone, and living with strangers was not going to be easy.

It wasn't the rules or the regulations that bothered me. The rules were actually very lenient, being that it was a home for first-time placements.

It was the lack of privacy that I couldn't stand. I couldn't retreat into my world anymore. There was no door on my bedroom, no locks on my closets or drawers, not even on the bathroom door. Nowhere for me to hide, which in turn meant I had no peace of mind.

I could be in the middle of a shower and *creeeek*. "Oops, I didn't know you were in here." Or I could be in the middle of changing my clothes when a female supervisor would walk into my bedroom.

Faced by these changes, I was going through hell.

One thing I really hated were the Sunday trips our group home took together. I was forced to go along with people I didn't want to be with, to a place I didn't want to go, when I just wanted to be left alone. This is how I felt, not just on Sundays, but every day.

I remember one trip we took to the Brooklyn Bridge. It was a walk across the bridge for a charity event. "Wear comfortable shoes," said the supervisors, "and don't forget your shorts, it'll be a hot one."

"Does everyone have to go?" I asked.

"Yes, everyone must go together and stay together."

Great, now my torment would begin.

This was my first weekend at the group home, so I did everything that I was told without question. I didn't want to seem like a troublemaker.

So I went along quietly. As everyone got on the train, the anxiety began to build inside of me. I could feel the eyes looking at me, like I was the prey of hungry lions. It seemed as though every time I would build up enough courage to look at one person, there would be a whole group looking back.

Finally, we arrived at the bridge. When we got off the train we were told to stick together. I pretended to walk with a group of guys from the group home until we got to the bridge.

But less than two minutes into the walk I disappeared. I walked leisurely away from everyone else. I began to walk faster and faster.

Before I knew it I was in a mini-sprint. Maybe deep down I was trying to run away from everybody.

I arrived at the end of the bridge long before anyone else. Once I did I simply sat down, put my head between my knees, and finally had some time alone.

Sure, there were people constantly passing back and forth, but I didn't care. I could finally just sit there and do nothing without anyone asking, "What's wrong with the new guy?" It was only a few minutes of being alone before everyone else arrived, but these few minutes alone were what kept me going.

So basically I ran from everyone for as long as I could. No one would get into my world no matter how hard they tried.

But I did talk to six of the seven boys that I was living with. Your occasional *hi's* and *bye's* and small talk.

They were all friendly. I was slightly older, so I guess they looked up to me a little. Sometimes I would go out to the store or to the park, and before I knew it, I had company. There were even times we got along really well, but I never let them get too close.

So they took it upon themselves to try to find out what was on my mind. All six of them tried to pry into my personal life. All six of them failed. There was no way I was going to let anyone get past my wall. Until one day when I got caught with my guard down.

A supervisor and I were having breakfast alone one day. No one else was awake yet. Then she suddenly asked, "Why are you here?" So I told her that I had family problems that I needed to get away from. Little did I know this would lead to the single most important conversation that I had ever had.

Turns out we talked that morning for at least two hours. Without even knowing it, she came into my life and related so well. For everything I told her, there was some sound, logical advice she had to give.

I let her know about the physical abuse that I had gone through at home. The supervisor simply replied, "Isn't that how your parents were brought up? Do you honestly think they hate you?"

I thought for a second and then I told her how it was affecting my school life negatively. She wisely replied again, "I know that there must be a lot on your mind. You should try talking about it more." Then she took a long, hard look at me and concluded: "That's what I'm here for."

So the next day I returned to her, asking for more advice. We talked again for what seemed like forever.

"Do you really think I belong in here?" I asked.

"No one really belongs in a group home," she said, "just think of it as an interval to your next step in life."

By the end of our conversation, I felt the weirdest feeling I had ever had. It was a calm, "light" feeling. I couldn't understand why I felt like that because I had never felt like that before. I did know that I liked it, though.

Before long, I figured it out. I tied together the feeling of inner tranquility to the casual conversations. Once I did, I began to speak a lot more often. I even got somewhat closer to the group home residents.

We all got along really well by the final week I was there. We went out together, played basketball, softball, and even hung out. We would sometimes go out at night and sit on the roof of the garage for an hour or so.

Although at first I didn't want to be friendly, I benefited greatly from the talking, playing, and joking around. It all helped in easing my tension.

Together with the help of the supervisors and my newly-made friends, I learned how to speak out to others. By the time I left the group home three weeks later, these people had made such a positive impact on my life that I have a hard time describing it with words. This gradual but steady change continued on through the next eleven months, while I was living in a foster home.

For some, going into care can be heart-wrenching, even petrifying. However, if you handle it correctly and give in just a little, you'll be surprised at what can be accomplished. I would like to thank the Graham-Windham foster care agency of Brooklyn for giving me my new beginning.

❏

Mohamed Khan, 17, spent eleven months in a foster home after the group home experience described above. He is now living with his biological family. He hopes to become a therapist and a writer. Of this story, he writes, "By speaking out, I let people know that I needed help finding myself. Now that I have, I'd like to help those who are still lost."

I WON'T ABUSE MY KIDS

Saretta Andrea Burkett

I t's a weekday evening. I'm sitting on top of my bed, sobbing profusely. Just received a beating from my mother. What did I do to deserve it? I can't really remember.

Sometimes I'd get beat if I talked back to grandma. Other times, for touching something in the house that didn't belong to me. Or for forgetting to clean out the tub after I'd used it.

Really didn't matter what I'd get beat for. At the end of some whippings, I'd sit on my bed and say to myself, *When I have kids, I'm never gonna beat them.*

Mother demanded that I take my punishment in dignity and silence. "Like a woman," she would sneer. Any yelping or whimpering from me would cause her to strike again. Beatings were endless, until I choked, literally, to hold down the screams.

You will read this, I'm sure, and conclude that I was a victim of abuse. But at the time, it wasn't obvious to either mother or me.

You see, mother thought children were victims of abuse only if they'd been molested sexually, beaten into unconsciousness, or abandoned in the streets. No, to mother I wasn't being abused. She was simply raising me the best way she knew how.

During my first year in the system, after tearful nights and weekly sessions with the resident therapist, I was able to acknowledge to myself that I had been abused. However, I wasn't aware that mother's abusive patterns were very much alive and growing within me.

In the group home I was known for my hot temper and quick, violent ways of ending disputes. Little mistakes made by the girls would send me flying into a hot rage. I'd cool off only after several doors had been kicked and a few glasses broken. Concerned counselors would pull me aside, but I waved away my actions as just "blowing off steam."

One Thanksgiving Day I visited my grandmother's house. (Also residing there are my mother, my aunt Lunette, and her ten-year-old son, my cousin Clyde.)

On this particular weekend, both Auntie Lunette and mother were at work. Grandmother and Clyde were home. After about an hour of chatting and watching television, grandma stepped away to take a shower, leaving me to tend to young Clyde.

Before leaving, she gave me specific instructions to call for her if Clyde misbehaved. "Don't give Saretta trouble, Clyde," she said, and went off.

Well, as soon as Clyde heard water running in the shower, he decided to turn the television from the Thanksgiving parade to the cartoon channel, which grandma had advised him not to do.

"Yo, Clyde," I said sternly, "chill with the TV."

In minutes, a matter as trivial as what television station to watch evolved into a major dispute, which Clyde ended with the words, "You're not my mother. I'm not listening to you."

I felt humiliated. Here I was, eighteen years old, being dictated to by someone eight years my junior. I wanted Clyde to listen. I wanted him to obey me. So I did to him what mother had done to me so many times before: I hit him across the face with the back of my hand.

In doing so, I was careful not to cause him too much pain, but enough to make him realize I was serious. He shouted in agony and rushed my legs with punches as hard as his little hands could throw.

"What?" I said, both shocked and angry that this ten-year-old had actually hit me back. In a moment, faster than it takes for a person to think, I grabbed the remote control and swung it at Clyde's head.

Everything happened so quickly. The remote dropped from my hand and my body trembled as I noticed blood streaming from a gash in Clyde's head.

"Oh my God oh my God oh my God oh my God oh my God

oh my God oh my God, Jesus, I didn't mean to hit you, Clyde!"

He was screaming at the top of his lungs. Never had he seen so much blood. I tried to subdue his screams and put my hands over his mouth, but Clyde shoved me away and yelled all the louder.

At this point, I was more worried about stopping the blood than keeping him quiet. Wads of red Kleenex tissue were strewn on the floor. In looking at the amount of blood this kid was shedding, I panicked: Clyde might need medical attention.

Grandma heard the screams and came running out of the shower, wet and dripping, clad only in a towel.

"Oh my gosh! I leave you with Clyde for one minute and this is what happens? Oh my gosh!"

She pulled him into the bathroom and was able to stop the bleeding. I walked back into grandma's room, stared out the window, blankly reflecting on what taken place in a matter of seconds. *My temper,* I said to myself, *I need help.*

Minutes later grandma came back, freshly clothed, along with Clyde. His face and neck were wiped clean of blood. There was nothing but a small Band-aid, smack dab across the center of his forehead.

I could only stand there and look at him. I had wanted him to be afraid of me just so he would obey. And now I had left a scar on him. Grandma split the blame between us: Clyde for not listening and me for hitting him.

But there was nothing she could say to rid me of my guilt. At first I was going to hang around until mother got home from work, but now I decided it wouldn't be such a good idea.

The subway ride from Brooklyn to my group home in lower Manhattan was a most agonizing one. I put on my Walkman in an attempt to forget what happened, but there was no distracting me. Echoes of Clyde's frightful screams filled my brain. I opened my hands and stared at them for a while, not quite believing that I had hurt a child, my own cousin, no less.

A couple of minutes prior to entering Marian Hall, my group home, I looked at my reflection in a car window and checked for any traces of tears. "I'm fine," I assured myself, choked up though I was. I walked into my floor and the area was bustling with activity, as is normal on a Saturday afternoon.

Before I could even duck and hide myself in my room, one of the girls called out, "Hey, Saretta, you got blood on your shirt."

That did it. The protective wall I'd built for myself was crumbling fast and I needed to talk. Barbara, the staff on duty at the time, pulled me to the patio where it was more private. Five cigarettes later, I spilled the beans. I told her everything: how I felt, what I did, and how sincerely sorry I was.

Barbara sympathized with me but did agree that I was in need of help, professional or otherwise. She also pointed out that my violent tendencies may have stemmed from the abuse I experienced as a child.

As mentioned at the start of this article, I did accept having been abused by my mother. But until now I hadn't accepted or even dealt with being a potential abuser of others.

It was somewhat disturbing to think that I was becoming exactly what I hated in my mother. Part of me wanted to remain in the comfort of denial, but I knew that minimizing the seriousness of the situation would lead to more expressions of violence.

One helpful outlet for me was self-help books. My choice was *Anxiety, Phobias & Panic: Taking Charge and Conquering Fear* by Reneau Z. Peurifoy.

It was comforting to see that someone had taken the time to write out what I had experienced and what I was feeling.

For example: in the first chapter entitled "What, Why, and How," Peurifoy talks about the general anxieties people suffer from and how they are linked to the abuse they experienced as children.

I was shocked to find that I possessed many of the traits that characterize someone as having high anxiety—namely, the excessive need for approval, extremely high expectations of self, and an excessive need to be in control.

But the scariest was yet to be found. In the following paragraphs, there was a list of family factors that led to a person having such a high-anxiety personality. I suffered from all the factors, including alcoholism in the family and a rigid belief system (meaning that your parents set up strict rules for everything, without room for compromise).

It was upsetting to see that I experienced more than one high-anxiety factor in my family. Most people have a hard time swallowing this new-found information.

While reading this book, I continued to see Ms. Hoffman, the therapist assigned to me at the group home. She was helpful for a time, but I needed to do more than talk about the problem and discuss the possible solutions. I had to apply these solutions to my life and practice them daily.

For example, during the last three weeks of school I had to put in a lot of study time. That meant either staying at the Chelsea Library until closing time or locking myself in my room.

I preferred to stay home and study. The problem was, I shared my space with two other sisters. So every five minutes or so, I had to get up from my desk to open the door for them, which eventually got annoying.

Rather than telling them to go to hell, I left the door open just a crack to avoid getting up. All was quiet on the western front until the girls turned up the volume on the television to watch "The Muppet Show."

At this point I could've dealt with this situation as I did with Clyde when I didn't get my way: by yelling at or even hitting the girls. And again, as with Clyde, I was experiencing an excessive need to be in control.

But unlike the incident with Clyde, I understood why I was angry. So I shoved down the temptation and shut the door that sectioned off the hallway from the living room, and things quieted down.

In dealing with anger, it is wise to not put yourself in situations that will upset you. I had to admit that if I had turned in my school assignments on time, I wouldn't have had to rush at the last minute and be an inconvenience to everyone. I had to acknowledge that I had responsibility for my anger.

Another productive outlet was journal writing. I didn't write entries at the end of the day as some might do, but during those times when the thought of shoving my fist down someone's throat was most tempting. In a month's time, not only was I able to analyze my feelings and pinpoint exactly what things would trigger off my fits of anger, but I sharpened my skills as a writer as well.

Even though I have made a sincere effort to curb my anger, it still comes out every now and then. One incident happened last summer when I entered a relationship with a sister (let's call her Lydia). Even before getting serious about this particular woman, I never thought there would come a time when I'd want to hurt her intentionally if she did something to aggravate me. Well, lo and behold.

It was a Saturday morning at her apartment, and I was downstairs by the washing machine sorting out our clothes. There was no one there but me.

"Saretta!" someone yelled and I jumped out of my skin. I turned around and Lydia was staring at me with a box of Bounce in her hands.

It wasn't her intention to frighten me. She had come to tell me that I had forgotten the fabric softener.

Well, I just didn't see it that way at the time. I was so angry that I raised a bottle and smashed it on the dryer. It was as if I'd been possessed.

Once again, I was scared of my reaction. I walked to the window and took a few deep breaths. I turned around to apologize to Lydia and she was gone. "I'm sorry," I said to the space where she once stood. "I'm sorry."

I went back to the apartment and she looked at me like I was a total stranger.

A few days after the incident, Lydia approached me with great concern. She feared that the next time I exploded, I would do worse—perhaps hit her.

I apologized and assured Lydia that I could never lay a finger on her in malice. But deep down I realized that just as I had not intended to hit Clyde with the remote control months earlier, it had happened. I wasn't too sure that it wouldn't happen again, but I felt I had a better chance of dealing with it.

Of course, as with the other situations, there were alternatives to smashing that bottle against the dryer.

One is using breathing techniques, one of the many methods Dr. Peurifoy lists at the end of each chapter that have really helped me in dealing with anger and phobias.

By the end of chapter two, I was able to internalize several methods of breathing that are very effective in calming oneself in stressful situations.

No matter what form of help you seek in dealing with anger, none will guarantee you an overnight solution. It's like writing with your left hand your whole life and suddenly deciding to switch to your right.

I still get angry. But there is relief in knowing that I'm doing something about it.

It's also good to know that in the near future, when it's my turn to raise children, I will have had some time to practice being human and more sensitive to the feelings of others.

❏

Saretta Andrea Burkett, 19, entered the system in 1992. She believes foster care should be a last resort, only after the fam-

ily has received all the help it needs: "If the parents are the ones perpetrating the violence, they should receive care and therapy. The same also for the children . . . We need to redefine abuse and communication issues." A skilled poet and photographer, Saretta was awarded a scholarship to attend Manhattanville College in the fall of 1994.

WRITING TAUGHT ME ABOUT MYSELF

Omar Sharif

O ne of the best things I learned from my foster mother, Ms. Bradley, is how to express my feelings through writing.

Before I lived with her, I never spoke to anyone about how I felt. I had no one to confide in, no one I could trust. I kept all my anger bottled up inside. My aunt and uncle never asked me how I was doing or what I was feeling. Keeping everything inside is not good, because after a while it starts to build up and bother you.

Every morning and every night I used to see Ms. Bradley write in a notebook. I was always curious to know what she was writing, so one day I asked her about it.

She told me it was a journal of her life, that she wrote about everything that happened throughout the day and whatever feelings came into her head.

"Omar," she said to me, "you can write about your anger."

She said that I would have to be honest with myself as I wrote, but that through writing I would be able to see where things went wrong in my life and how I could begin to change.

I doubted what she said because I had never seen anyone solve problems by writing about them. But Ms. Bradley explained how writing had helped her deal with her own mother not wanting her when she was a child. She said it took her ten years to get over her feelings about her mom and the way she did it was through writing. When she told me this, I believed her one hundred percent.

I began to write because I had lost faith in people. I had learned to trust Ms. Bradley, but when I didn't want to talk to her or anyone else, I would write down my feelings in my book.

I would write every night before I went to bed. Sometimes I would write for hours. My best writing came when I was angry or upset. Sometimes I wrote about bad memories. Then I would rip the paper up, throw it on the floor, and stomp on it. That was my way of getting it off my chest. I would feel so relieved whenever I finished writing my feelings.

Through writing I realized why I had certain problems. I used to start fires in elementary school and I never understood why. Through writing I saw that I had a lot of anger and resentment because I couldn't live with my pops, and that I started fires to relieve that anger.

The best way to understand your feelings is to write about them. It can be even better than talking because you don't have to confide in anyone. You don't have to worry about anyone knowing your business, because whatever you write is for your eyes only. By understanding who you are through writing, you can help yourself to a better life.

❏

Omar Sharif, 20, is also the author of "My Foster Mother Is My Best Friend" and "How I Lived a Double Life" in this collection.

A VACATION
FROM MR. HOPE

Wunika Hicks

My heart hurt as I watched my mother, a mother of strength, look so powerless as my brother and I rode off into the night with the BCW workers at our side. My mind drifted off as I watched the neighborhood school children run inside my favorite candy store, the only one on the whole block that sold Now & Laters with three in a pack for a nickel.

It was funny how we were in pain, but the world never stopped for us, it still moved on. I guess you could say it's just like the moon and the stars—you want them to shine forever, but then they disappear and you're left hoping for tomorrow.

"Wunika, how are you, girl? You doing good in school? How's your brother David? I want you to know that we love you. And never worry about anything because we're family, and family sticks together."

I remember hearing my aunts say that last sentence a lot, so much that I believed them, but cradling my brother in my arms and looking into his eyes as he watched the unfamiliar faces around him in the car, I had to wonder if all the things my aunts said were true.

My brother and I ended up in a foster home together. Life wasn't so bad living there. I had hope in my heart and mind, hope that I'd pretty soon be back with my mother or aunts (whoever came first). I just knew it would be soon, and I had the weekly visits to my aunt's house to prove it. I imagined myself actually moving back with my family and saying to my foster mom: "I'm moving, bye-bye, I promise to keep in touch, love ya."

Baam! My visits to my aunt were stopped, my dreams were shattered.

There seemed to be some sort of problem between my mother and my aunt. My mother felt threatened by my aunt's responsibility for my brother and me. All I was now allowed were visits at the agency, and the only one who visited me was my mother. And when she did come, she came with a little bit of hope, but I guess it wasn't much because pretty soon she stopped visiting, too.

After my real family disappeared, all I had was my foster family and the Lord knew that if it wasn't real, I didn't want it.

My foster mother used to say: "Beggars can't be choosers." I didn't consider myself a beggar, so I knew I could be choosy, even if it meant denying the only family I now had.

As year after year passed, I lost all touch with my real family. Guess I sorta kinda got used to my foster family. It was good having people care for me. But I still had a pinch of hope hidden somewhere in me to be with my real family, and I was still searching for it.

I should have known not to let my foster family get to know me. I should've kept my guard up as planned, 'cause they weren't my family.

Yeah, one day it was time to go, the old lady was kicking me out after five years over some differences of opinion. It hurt to be put out again. First I was taken away from my mother, and now I was kicked out by a lady who I called "mother" because that was the role she took on.

I could only assume I was the one with the problem. But I sure wished the hope that was hidden inside me would show its face, because I surely needed it.

I was thirteen when I arrived in my second foster home, and boy, was I something! As I look back, I can only laugh. I walked around that lady's home as if I owned it.

I never said "good morning," and back at my first foster mama's house that was enough to get a whuppin'.

Sooo what! I could care less. She wasn't no blood of mine, just another lady tryin' to play mother, a mother I didn't want 'cause she wasn't real, she wasn't blood. I still had that hope, and I just knew I would find it soon, I just knew it.

But everything seemed to go wrong. I wasn't at my new foster home for a month before they talked about my brother getting adopted by parents who didn't even know him.

That hurt, because where would that leave me? I didn't want him to have parents who had to pay fees to get custody of him. Shoot, he wasn't nobody's property! He was a person, and he, WE, were supposed to get back home to our family.

After my brother was adopted (you'd think they would have listened to me after all the tears and protesting), I could say I was truly alone. I had no family whatsoever, only jive turkeys playing a role they were paid to act. Shoot! If CWA knew what I knew, they'd hire better actors!

The years flew by and I still hadn't found my family or vice versa, and my brother was in a sealed adoption. I hadn't seen him since he was taken away, and if you ask me, that was the way my agency liked it—less paperwork, less confusion. I'm sure their hearts were content.

I just went on living in my world of hope. I tried to accept life as it was: my real family was gone. It was hard to swallow. My mind accepted it, but my heart knew something different.

I gradually adjusted to my second foster mother. I had no choice. I began to hate the blood relatives I had once yearned for. I blamed them for my situation.

I blamed my mother also, but not as much as my relatives. I knew that the hopes my mother whispered in my ears when she used to come to the agency were nothing but hopes. I had spent my early years with my mother, so I knew what she was able to do and not able.

But thinking back to the family visits I had years ago, when my relatives would whisper those same dreams, I remembered how my mind filled with belief, how my heart beat with anticipation. I felt my hopes would come true, because I didn't know what my relatives were incapable of. They gave me more hope, so I had more anger for them when those hopes didn't come true.

Going on with my life, I noticed that writing was something I enjoyed, so that's exactly what I did. I wrote poetry, short stories about my relationships with guys, and personal stories about my life.

Well, wouldn't you know that after ten years in foster care, my real family found me through my writing! I was interviewed by *New York Newsday* for a story about *Foster Care Youth United*. They interviewed me because of a story I had written about my adopted brother.

Newsday's story hit the stands two days later. And guess what?

Exactly two days after that, my relatives found me after seeing my photo in the paper. My uncle called me up at my writing job and asked for his niece.

Honey, ya shoulda been there to see the Kool-Aid smile on my face. Chile, my hopes had finally been found! My hopes were them—my blood family.

Well, I'm sure you can imagine what went on the day of my discovery. Yeah, I saw my relatives, my aunts, uncles, cousins, and even my mother. My mother was living good now, married, and had an income. She was living in Texas, but ran up to New York when my relatives told her I'd been found.

When she saw me for the first time in ten years, she held my face in her hands and said: "Look at you, you've grown up, I thought of you all the time. I hope you forgive me, I was just going through so much."

I told her basically the same things. I just wished that none of this had happened to us. My mother was real hurt when I told her my brother was adopted.

"*Where is he? Who has him?*" she asked me in so much pain that I wished I could've given her some answers.

Yup, that was surely a day I'll never forget—all of those hugs and kisses, those "I love you's" and "I missed you's."

It was around then that I started smellin' my behind. *Chile,* now that I had contact with my real family, I put my foster mama through a lot.

I ran away to my blood mother in Texas for a week and a half. I went there to find a mother with a new life, someone I didn't know. She wasn't as wild as she was in the past. Instead, she was soft-spoken and sweet. It was a lot to get used to and there was a lot of time to make up.

Just my luck—them people from BCW were on my AWOL trail, so I had to come back home to my old foster mom. But I didn't care about her 'cause I wanted *my* family, and now I thought I finally had them.

Shoot, they were buying me clothes, handing me food, and giving me their undivided attention. I thought I had it made, and who wouldn't? If you did that for a homeless person, he'd think the same exact things I thought. But as I look back, I ask myself: *Who pays you to think?*

Well, like I said before, I wasn't no beggar, so I could be choosy—and I chose my blood over them other ones. It's funny how the past repeats itself, and if you're reading my story closely enough, you know exactly what I'm tryin to say . . .

Yup! It was time for me to pack those bags again. I had to move to a group home 'cause my foster mother and I had a difference of opinion.

I was almost eighteen, too old to be movin' from place to place. I started to feel that ole hope—yup, sure enough, he was knockin' at my damn door again. As I look back, I sure wished he'd have left me alone, but he didn't.

My mama always said, "A man will only do what ya let him." Well, *my family* is all I thought of as I packed my little bags with my foster mammy lookin' on. I even told her I didn't care about her, I only cared about *"My* family." Lordy, Lordy, I shoulda known.

I went straight into a group home, me and Mr. Hope. I called my relatives all the time. When I got lucky, they even called me back.

My mother wanted me to come back home with her to stay, but I wouldn't go. After all those years of physical abuse from her, it was really scary to take the chance of living with her again. Even though she seemed to have changed for the better, I still wondered if she was really a new person or just acting. Even though she had a house and a car, I wanted them other jive turkeys—my aunts, my uncles, and my cousins, because I felt they were much safer than my mother.

Well, to make a long story short, I've been in this group home for six months. Mosta them were spent with you know who . . . Mr. Hope. We were waiting for my relatives to take us home, but none of them suckers made a move. And boy, did I cry for them to take me home! Mr. Hope, he was still with me by my side durin' it all, cheerin' me on, whisperin' sweet nothings in my ear, and makin' me look like the fool I was.

Till this day, I question why I didn't look at things for what they were. Why did I have to play it up to be something else? Why couldn't I realize earlier that my relatives had a life of their own without me? That the family I once had was no longer there? And most importantly, why did I put such an emphasis on "blood family"?

I just thought that I'd let ya'll know that I've taken a vacation from Mr. Hope. A lot of people thought I was getting too serious with him and they said that I should wake up and start dating this new guy, Mr. Reality (he was always tryin' to talk to me).

So I gave him a try and would you believe I'm in love with him? Chile, chile, chile, Mr. Reality saved my life and the Lord only knows how thankful I am.

Mr. Hope, yeah, he still be trying to get into my life, and at times I'm tempted to go back, but I got Reality, so I don't need him no more.

I hurt a lot of people messin' around with ole Hope. Shoot, don't get me wrong—Hope is good, but it shouldn't be forever. There must be a time that you wake up to you know who . . . (Reality's my man, but there's enough ta go around. I was never the jealous type anyway.)

The past does have a tendency to repeat itself, but you can change it if you try. I've decided to leave the group home and go back to my foster mother.

I made a mistake getting kicked out of my first home and I'm sorry to say I'll never be able to go back. My first foster mother passed away, God bless her soul. I wish I could've been able to acknowledge my faults while she was still alive, but I'm glad that I've gotten this far. I can't make the same mistake twice, 'cause you never know when my second foster mother may go off the face of the earth, too.

But at least when she does go, she'll know what I'm about. Chile, not everyone gets to know what I'm about. Even the ones who do, don't know all—they just like to think they do. I guess I butter 'em up like that to make them feel good. Shoot, you can't have people feelin' like they dumb all the time!

I remember the sayin' "Blood is thicker than water." In my case, that's not true. Don't get me wrong—I will always love my biological family. They just can't supply me with the security that I want. But both of my foster homes treated me well and I thank them with all my heart. They were and are my *family*. I'm glad I've finally realized that.

❏

Wunika Hicks is also the author of three other pieces in this collection: "I Lost My Brother to Adoption," "She'll Always Be My Mother," and "Sista on the Run (From the Past)."

MESSAGES
FROM THE WRITERS

"I hope after reading this book you will be better able to understand kids in foster care and will look at them without negative stereotypes. This book shows that kids have a voice, that we have concerns and feelings, and we hope you listen to them. I hope you share what you've learned with others who haven't read it."

—CRAIG JAFFE

❑   ❑   ❑

"I feel excited and happy that my work was included in this book. I hope that you won't look at the painful things I wrote about as being bad but look at them as things that helped me become the person I am today. I hope adults and not just children will realize what kids go through. Behind every dark path there's a light, and the past doesn't have to stop you from excelling."

—WUNIKA HICKS

❏   ❏   ❏

"I feel honored to be published in this book. I hope you have a better sense of what foster care is and how we perceive it first-hand. Hopefully people will pay more attention to foster care, learn more about it, and get involved: donate money, take kids in as foster parents. Just don't read this book and forget all about us, because we are people, too, and are finally getting our voices heard after so many years of silence. Don't just sit there and feel sorry for us: stand up and do something about it."

—LENNY JONES

❏   ❏   ❏

"The book was a great opportunity to have our words spoken and to help others with our articles. There are so many books about foster care, but this one is different because it's from kids in care. The articles aren't what people think we should write but are based on our real experiences, the issues behind the walls put up by administrators and social workers in this field. I hope more parents will get involved in helping their kids in foster care, that administrators will train the staff to work with us better emotionally, and that those reading my article will know they're not alone."

—TIEYSHA MCVAY

❏   ❏   ❏

"Hopefully, a lot more attention will be paid to foster care. I can't say specifically what might change as a result of this book,

but once you have everything out in the open, things have to eventually change. I hope you enjoyed reading this."

—CARLFORD WADLEY

❏   ❏   ❏

"The pieces in this book will play a critical role in dismantling the wall of stigma that surrounds youth in care. I sincerely hope that people will walk away from this reading experience understanding that we are victims, not perpetrators, in the dysfunctional family. More importantly, we've used the past as a blueprint that will hopefully prevent us from repeating the family mistakes that landed us in the system to begin with."

—SARETTA ANDREA BURKETT

GLOSSARY OF SLANG

This key to common slang terms used in this book was compiled by Shawan Raheem Samuels.

All that: great or superior, as in "She thinks she's all that."
Ball, ballin': playing basketball.
Beef: a conflict.
Blow up someone's spot: to give away a secret; to expose.
Blunt: marijuana rolled in a cigar.
Boogie Down: the Bronx.
Booms: marijuana.
Bouncing: moving or leaving.
Break night: to hang out until the next morning.
Buddah or buddha: marijuana.
Buggin': acting crazy.
Bumrush: to rush at something; to crash, as in "bumrush a party."
Bus' a cap: shoot a gun.
C.I.: a cigarette.
Chill: to hang out or relax.
Chocolate Thai: a type of marijuana.
Cop: to purchase or acquire something.
Crew: a group of people or friends, sometimes a gang.
Crib: apartment or house.

Dead, to dead: to stop something or to leave something alone, as in "Dead the beef."

Dead presidents: money.

Digits: phone numbers.

Dime bag: $10 bag of marijuana.

Dipped: being fashionable.

Dis: to disrespect, to insult.

Dope: fine, great.

Down: to be a part of something, to be accepted.

Five-O, or 5-0: the police, after "Hawaii 5-0."

Flip a script: start a fight.

Flippin': the act of doing something; to fight or do something crazy.

Flow: to rhyme or rap.

For self: do something for yourself; in your own interest.

Forty: a 40 oz. bottle of beer or malt liquor.

Front or frontin': the act of deceiving; to put on a front.

Funds: money.

Gear: clothing.

Ghost: to leave, to depart, as in "I'm ghost."

Heads: a crowd of people.

Hiney: a Heineken beer.

Hit off: to give.

Honey: a woman.

Hood: the neighborhood of someone from the streets.

Hooky parties: parties held while cutting school.

Joint: a gun; also marijuana cigarette.

Lounge: to take it easy or to stop doing something, as in "You gots to lounge on the booms tip."

Mad: a lot of something.

Makin' mine: making money for yourself.

Money Makin': Manhattan.

Munk: to rob someone.

Nickel bag: $5 bag of marijuana.

N-gga: a male of any race.

On the low or down low; on the D.L.: keeping something a secret.

On the regulah: doing something often.

Open: high from drugs.

Packing: possessing a gun.

Parlay: to relax, to hang out, to chill.

Peeps: friends, after "people."

Phat: good or great; expressing the feeling of liking something.

Phillie: a cigar filled with marijuana (see *Blunt*).

Play: to fool or deceive, as "I thought this girl liked me, but I got played."

Posse: a crew or gang.

Pound: to knock fists in greeting.

Props: respect.

Re-up: to buy drugs to resell.

Riffin': complaining, arguing.

Rock: crack cocaine.

Roughneck or ruffneck: a rowdy person from the streets.

Sellout: coward.

Skunk: a type of marijuana.

Slay: to disrespect; to foil someone's plans.

Snappin': cracking jokes; clever insults.

Snuffed: sucker punched; to get hit by surprise.

Steel: a gun.

Step to: confront.

Stog: a cigarette.

Strapped: possessing a gun.

Stressin' my pockets: spending more than you can afford.

Swingin' a little somethin': to have a relationship with someone.

Tag: a nickname; also a graffiti artist's signature.

Tip: a certain subject or area, as in, "I know you got skills on the ball tip."

Whining: a sexual reggae dance involving winding your hips in synch with your partner.

You go, girl: praise or acknowledgement of achievement; feminist slogan.

RESOURCES

If you want to learn more about foster children or foster care in general, contact the following organizations:

NATIONAL FOSTER PARENT ASSOCIATION
908 Glaizewood Court
Takoma Park, MD 20912
301–270–1000

NATIONAL ASSOCIATION OF FORMER FOSTER CHILDREN
P.O. Box 874
Wall Street Station
New York, NY 10268–0874
212–332–0078

NORTH AMERICAN COUNCIL ON ADOPTABLE CHILDREN
970 Raymond Avenue
Suite 106
St. Paul, MN 55114–1149
612–644–3036

CHILD WELFARE LEAGUE OF AMERICA
440 First St., NW, Suite 310
Washington, DC 20001-2085
202-638-2952

CHILDREN'S DEFENSE FUND
25 E St., NW
Washington, DC 20001
202–628–8787

NATIONAL COURT APPOINTED SPECIAL ADVOCATE
ASSOCIATION (CASA)
2722 Eastlake Avenue E.
Suite 220
Seattle, WA 98102
206–328–8588

You can also contact your local department of human or social services.

To find out more about *Foster Care Youth United*, or for subscription information, write or call:

FOSTER CARE YOUTH UNITED
Youth Communication
144 West 27th St.
New York, NY 10001
212–242–3270 (telephone)
212–242–7057 (fax)

SUBJECT GUIDE

Abuse and Neglect

    Questions Without Answers   3
    I Lost My Brother to Adoption   30
    She'll Always Be My Mother   34
    Finding a Father in the System   64
    Why I'm Better Off in Foster Care   73
    Staying with the Hurt   171
    My Family Secret   174
    Therapy Changed My Life   180
    I Won't Abuse *My* Kids   197

Adoption

    My Foster Mother Is My Best Friend   25
    I Lost My Brother to Adoption   30
    Sista on the Run (From the Past)   68
    A Vacation from Mr. Hope   206

AIDS and HIV

    Questions Without Answers   3
    How I Made Peace with the Past   185

Alcoholism

Questions Without Answers   3
Six Months on the Run from the BCW   9
My Crew Was My Family   39
Facing the Problem   190

Bereavement

How I Made Peace with the Past   185

Biological Parents

Questions Without Answers   3
Six Months on the Run from the BCW   9
I Lost My Brother to Adoption   30
She'll Always Be My Mother   34
Sista on the Run (From the Past)   68
Why I'm Better Off in Foster Care   73
Is Stealing My Addiction?   143
My Family Secret   174
How I Made Peace with the Past   185
I Won't Abuse *My* Kids   197
A Vacation from Mr. Hope   206

Conflict Resolution

Peer Pressure and Me   97
Phat Flows, Honeys, and the Booms   147
From Fighter to Friend   167

Dating

Why No One Knows I'm a Foster Child   125
Keeping It on the Down Low   128
What They Say Behind Our Backs   131
Kicked Out Because I Was Gay   135
My Friend Marisol   139
Phat Flows, Honeys, and the Booms   147
My Family Secret   174

Depression

Six Months on the Run from the BCW   9
A Three-Point Shooter   107
Facing the Problem   190
A Loner in the Group Home   193

Drug Addiction

Questions Without Answers   3
My Crew Was My Family   39
Peer Pressure and Me   97
Is Stealing My Addiction?   143
Phat Flows, Honeys, and the Booms   147

Foster Parents

My Foster Mother Is My Best Friend   25
Sista on the Run (From the Past)   68
Why No One Knows I'm a Foster Child   125
Kicked Out Because I Was Gay   135
Writing Taught Me About Myself   204
A Vacation from Mr. Hope   206

Foster Homes

My Foster Mother Is My Best Friend   25
Sista on the Run (From the Past)   68
Why No One Knows I'm a Foster Child   125
Kicked Out Because I Was Gay   135
Writing Taught Me about Myself   204
A Vacation from Mr. Hope   206

Gays and Lesbians

Kicked Out Because I Was Gay   135
My Friend Marisol   139

Group Homes

My Day in the Group Home   61
Finding a Father in the System   64
Why I'm Better Off in Foster Care   73
Can the Counselors Keep a Secret?   76
Making a New Family   78
Why Are You Doing This, Mr. Jones?   83
How I Became a Stronger Mother   93
Peer Pressure and Me   97
Kicked to the Curb at Twenty-One   100
My Group Home Scapegoat   105
A Three-Point Shooter   107
How I Lived a Double Life   121
Keeping It on the Down Low   128
My Friend Marisol   139
Is Stealing My Addiction?   143
From Fighter to Friend   167
My Family Secret   174
Therapy Changed My Life   180
A Loner in the Group Home   193
I Won't Abuse *My* Kids   197

Group Home Staff

My Day in the Group Home   61
Finding a Father in the System   64
Why I'm Better Off in Foster Care   73
Can the Counselors Keep a Secret?   76
Why Are You Doing This, Mr. Jones?   83
How I Became a Stronger Mother   93
Peer Pressure and Me   97
Kicked to the Curb at Twenty-One   100
A Three-Point Shooter   107
Keeping It on the Down Low   128
My Friend Marisol   139
Is Stealing My Addiction?   143
From Fighter to Friend   167
My Family Secret   174
Therapy Changed My Life   180
A Loner in the Group Home   193
I Won't Abuse *My* Kids   197

Independent Living

    Kicked to the Curb at Twenty-One   100

Peer Counseling/Group Therapy

    Why I'm Better Off in Foster Care   73
    How I Became a Stronger Mother   93
    Staying with the Hurt   171
    My Family Secret   174

Peer Pressure

    Six Months on the Run from the BCW   9
    My Crew Was My Family   39
    Peer Pressure and Me   97
    My Group Home Scapegoat   105
    Phat Flows, Honeys, and the Booms   147
    From Fighter to Friend   167

Peers, Relations with

    Six Months on the Run from the BCW   9
    My Crew Was My Family   39
    My Day in the Group Home   61
    Making a New Family   78
    How I Became a Stronger Mother   93
    Peer Pressure and Me   97
    My Group Home Scapegoat   105
    A Three-Point Shooter   107
    How I Lived a Double Life   121
    Why No One Knows I'm a Foster Child   125
    Keeping It on the Down Low   128
    What They Say Behind Our Backs   131
    My Friend Marisol   139
    Phat Flows, Honeys, and the Booms   147
    Who's the Real "Problem Child"?   155
    From Fighter to Friend   167
    Staying with the Hurt   171
    My Family Secret   174
    A Loner in the Group Home   193
    I Won't Abuse *My* Kids   197

Rape

Why Are You Doing This, Mr. Jones?   83
My Family Secret   174

Runaways

Six Months on the Run from the BCW   9
My Crew Was My Family   39
Sista on the Run (From the Past)   68
Therapy Changed My Life   180

Sexual Abuse

She'll Always Be My Mother   34
Sista on the Run (From the Past)   68
Why I'm Better Off in Foster Care   73
My Family Secret   174
Therapy Changed My Life   180

Sexuality

Six Months on the Run from the BCW   9
Why Are You Doing This, Mr. Jones?   83
Kicked Out Because I Was Gay   135
My Friend Marisol   139
Phat Flows, Honeys, and the Booms   147
I'm the Mommy Now   151
My Family Secret   174

Siblings, Relations with

Questions Without Answers   3
I Lost My Brother to Adoption   30
She'll Always Be My Mother   34
Finding a Father in the System   64
Why No One Knows I'm a Foster Child   125
Who's the Real "Problem Child"?   155
Therapy Changed My Life   180
How I Made Peace with the Past   185
A Vacation from Mr. Hope   206

Social Workers

Six Months on the Run from the BCW   9
I Lost My Brother to Adoption   30
Why Are You Doing This, Mr. Jones?   83
Phat Flows, Honeys, and the Booms   147
How I Made Peace with the Past   185

Stigma of Being a Foster Child

Sista on the Run (From the Past)   68
Can the Counselors Keep a Secret?   76
How I Lived a Double Life   121
Why No One Knows I'm a Foster Child   125
Keeping It on the Down Low   128
What They Say Behind Our Backs   131
Kicked Out Because I Was Gay   135
Who's the Real "Problem Child"?   155

Teenage Parents

Why Are You Doing This, Mr. Jones?   83
How I Became a Stronger Mother   93
I'm the Mommy Now   151
Staying with the Hurt   171

Therapy

Is Stealing My Addiction?   143
My Family Secret   174
Therapy Changed My Life   180
I Won't Abuse *My* Kids   197

Writing as Therapy

I Won't Abuse *My* Kids   197
Writing Taught Me about Myself   204

ACKNOWLEDGMENTS

We conceived the idea of a foster care magazine in the late 1980s, when New York City's crack epidemic was fueling a dramatic resurgence in the foster care population. Like many good ideas, however, it languished for lack of funding.

In October 1991 David Tobis, an old friend and child advocate, called to tell us that he was representing a new foundation interested in child welfare reform. Our idea of creating a magazine which would provide a voice to teens in the system fit with David's conviction that a client voice is an essential element in system reform. Through the Child Welfare Fund he provided us a planning grant and several subsequent grants, without which *Foster Care Youth United* would never have been possible.

Since then many other funders have supported this magazine: The Pinkerton Foundation, the WKBJ Partnership Foundation, The Edna McConnell Clark Foundation, the Spunk Fund, the Lavanburg-Corner House, The Rita J. and Stanley H. Kaplan Foundation, the Edward Hazen Foundation, Citibank, the New York Foundation, and the East New York Savings Bank. We applaud their commitment to improving the lives of young people in foster care, and are deeply grateful for their support.

Foster Care Youth United is published by Youth Communication, and the magazine would never get out the door without the collaboration and contributions of the Youth Communication staff. Sean Chambers worked as assistant editor on the magazine during our 1994 and 1995 summer writing workshops and Duffie Cohen was assistant editor in the 1995 summer workshop. We owe a special debt of gratitude to Giselle Benatar, who volunteered as assistant editor of *Foster Care Youth United* from October 1994 to June 1995. Other Youth Communication editors—Phil Kay, Andrea Estepa, and Vivian Louie—have also made contributions to the development of the magazine.

Tom Brown, the administrative director at Youth Communication, writes a newsletter to accompany each issue of *FCYU* which is filled with suggestions for using the magazine with teens. He also plays a key role in keeping the magazine financially afloat through fundraising and subscription management. Efrain Reyes skillfully executes the desktop publishing and design of each issue and maintains the cantankerous batch of computers in our newsroom.

Nearly two years of planning, recruiting, and teaching elapsed between our initial discussions about this project with David Tobis and publication of the premiere issue. During that time we talked to dozens of people inside and outside of the system to gauge the prospects for our proposed youth magazine. We extend our heartfelt thanks to Karolyn Gould, of the South Bronx Human Development Organization, who helped educate us about the system and provided our initial mailing list, and to Carl Mazza, of Louise Wise Services, who introduced us to many of the Independent Living Coordinators who have become our most important distributors. Other people who provided invaluable assistance during the planning process include Gary Mallon, John Courtney, Barbara Christian, Matt Meyer, Sr. Mary Geraldine, Rachel De Aragon, Paul Jensen, E. P. Jones, and Steve Cohen. And a shout out to the young women of St. Helena's Residence, a Good Shepherd Services group home, and to the other young people in care with whom we discussed the idea for this project. Their enthusiasm helped vanquish our doubts that teens in care would want to read a peer-written magazine and inspired us to push forward with this project.

Recruiting our first teen writers was very difficult. When we had little to show but a good idea, several people in the system went out of their way to identify young people who they knew had important ideas to share with their peers. Our thanks to Isidore Chevat, Sonia Diaz, James Edell, Karen Eubanks, Barbara Hagood, Angelique Leone, Larry Litoff, and Steve Parker for sending us many of the talented writers whose work appears in this book.

Once we began publishing, CWA Commissioner Robert Little and his staff were strong supporters within the system. Countless others have provided valuable feedback and support, including Brenda McGowan, Diana Autin, Betsy Krebs and the Youth Advocacy Center, and Kathy Mallow. Your support means more to us than you know. And we would especially like to thank Kathryn Conroy of the Columbia University School of Social Work for organizing a focus group of key subscribers to evaluate the magazine after the first year.

Everyone who has contributed to this project has shown great faith in the ability of young people in foster care to articulate their concerns. That faith gratifies and inspires us.

KEITH HEFNER
AL DESETTA

ABOUT YOUTH COMMUNICATION

Youth Communication is a nonprofit youth development program located in New York City, whose mission is to teach writing, journalism, and leadership skills. The teenagers we train, most of whom are New York City public high school students, become writers for our two teen-written publications, *New Youth Connections*, a general interest youth magazine, and *Foster Care Youth United*, a magazine for young people in foster care.

Youth Communication was founded in 1980 by Keith Hefner in response to a nationwide study which found that the high school press was characterized by censorship, mediocrity, and racial exclusion. Hefner has won a Charles H. Revson Fellowship at Columbia University and the Luther P. Jackson Excellence in Education Award from the New York Association of Black Journalists for his work at Youth Communication, and in 1989 he won a MacArthur "genius" Fellowship.

Each year, more than one hundred young people participate in Youth Communication's school-year and summer journalism workshops. They come from every corner of New York City, and the vast majority are African American, Latino, or Asian. The teen staff members work under the direction of several full-time adult editors in our Manhattan offices, which are equipped with two newsrooms, a score of computers, two darkrooms, an art department, and a desktop publishing and production department.

Teachers, counselors, social workers, and other adults circulate our magazines to young people in their classes and after-school youth programs.

They distribute 60,000 copies of *New Youth Connections* each month during the school year, and 10,000 bimonthly copies of *Foster Care Youth United*. Teachers frequently tell us that teens in their classes—including students who are ordinarily resistant to reading—clamor for these publications. For our teen writers, the opportunity to reach their peers with important self-help information, and with accurate portrayals of their lives, motivates them to create powerful stories.

Running a strong youth development program while also producing quality teen magazines requires a balance between a process that is sensitive to the complicated lives and emotions of the teen participants, and one that is intellectually rigorous. We sustain that balance in the writing/teaching/editing relationship, which is the core of our program.

Our teaching and editorial process begins with discussions between adult editors and the teen staff, during which they seek to discover the stories that are most important to each teen writer and that will also appeal to a significant segment of our reading public.

Once topics have been chosen, students begin the process of crafting their stories. For a personal story, that means revisiting events in one's past to understand their significance for the future. For a commentary, it means developing a logical and persuasive argument. For a reported story, it means gathering information through research and interviews. Students look inward and outward as they try to make sense of their experiences and the world around them, and find the points of intersection between personal and social concerns. That process can take a few weeks, or a few months. Stories frequently go through four, five, or more drafts as students work on their stories under the guidance of editors in the same way that any published writer does.

Many of the students who walk through our doors have uneven skills as a result of poor education, living under extremely stressful conditions, or coming from homes where English is a second language. Yet, to complete their stories, they must successfully perform a wide range of activities, including writing and rewriting, reading, discussion, reflection, research, interviewing, and typing. They must work as members of a team, and they must accept a great deal of individual responsibility. They learn to read subway maps, verify facts, and cope with rejection. They engage in explorations of truthfulness and fairness. They meet deadlines. They must develop the audacity to believe that they have something important to say, and the humility to recognize that saying it well is not a process of instant gratification but usually requires a long, hard struggle through many discussions and much rewriting.

It would be impossible to teach these skills and dispositions as separate, disconnected topics, like grammar, ethics, or assertiveness training. However, we find that students make rapid progress when they are learning skills within the context of an inquiry that is personally significant to them, and which they think will benefit their peers.

Writers usually participate in our program for one semester, though some stay much longer. Years later, many of them report that working here was a turning point in their lives—that it helped them acquire the confidence and skills that they needed for success in their subsequent education and careers. Scores of our graduates have overcome tremendous obstacles to become journalists, writers, and novelists. Hundreds more are working in law, teaching, business, and other careers.

Foster Care Youth United, from which all of the narratives in this book have been culled, was originally founded to give a voice to the nearly 50,000 young people in foster care in New York City. Conceived and planned by Keith Hefner and by founding editor Al Desetta, the magazine began bimonthly publication in June 1993. It now has subscribers in forty-five states.

Though young people in foster care face issues common to all young people, they experience them through the filter of separation from their parents. The magazine is designed to help young people in care share their special concerns with each other, and to make those concerns available to policy-makers and service providers. We hope that by accurately portraying the lives of foster children the magazine also will help to destigmatize the experience of being in care. That is an essential prerequisite for improving the system and the lives of the young people living in it.

ABOUT THE EDITOR

Al Desetta, founding editor of *Foster Care Youth United,* has worked at Youth Communication since 1985. He has served as editor of *New Youth Connections,* the organization's general interest magazine for teenagers, as instructor in its juvenile prison writing project, and as director of its teacher development program. In 1990, he was awarded a Charles H. Revson Fellowship at Columbia University.